CHARACTER AND MOTIVE IN SHAKESPEARE

CHARACTER AND MOTIVE IN SHAKESPEARE

SOME RECENT APPRAISALS EXAMINED

By

J. I. M. STEWART

Student of Christ Church, Oxford

NEW YORK
BARNES & NOBLE INC.
Publishers · Booksellers · Since 1873

First published 1949
New impression 1959
Paperback edition 1965
New impression 1966

Printed in Great Britain by Butler & Tanner Ltd
Frome and London

PREFACE

Will all great *Neptunes* Ocean wash this blood
Cleane from my Hand? no: this my Hand will rather
The multitudinous Seas incarnadine,
Making the Greene one, Red.

For Alexander Pope this of Macbeth's is stuff too sorry even
for an unlettered dramatist in a rude age; only interpolation by
players yet more unlettered can explain it; and if we want to
arrive at approximately what Shakespeare wrote we shall print

No, this my hand will rather
Make the green ocean red.

And to Johnson, as to Dryden before him, the Elizabethan age
was at only one remove from an infancy of language, and offered
therefore a climate essentially ungenial to any mature poetic art:
the public for which Shakespeare wrote, Johnson declares, had
more skill in pomps or processions than in poetical language.[1]
But in these judgments there are almost certainly operative the
prejudices of the period. In maintaining that Shakespeare's
poetry—and the poetry of the later Elizabethan and the Jacobean
drama in general—was crude and limited in comparison with
its own the eighteenth century had hold of the wrong end of the
stick. For the Elizabethan verbal sensibility was more subtle
than the Augustan, and in rejecting Shakespearian rhetoric the
contemporaries of Johnson were turning down an instrument
too complex for their understanding.

There is a lesson in this. It is unwise to maintain absolutely
that this or that aspect of Shakespeare's art is crude—or, indeed,
that the materials upon which he refined were altogether so.
To-day some critics vary Johnson's dictum by declaring that the
public for whom Shakespeare wrote had more skill in poetical
language than in human nature; and they maintain that Shakespeare was concerned less with the well-springs of human action

than with giving poetical integument and theatrical impetus to matter that remains essentially sensational and rude. The following essays would suggest that to regard Shakespeare in this way is often to make something like Pope's mistake over again. It was Pope's poetic that was narrow, and not Shakespeare's; it is the critics' psychology that is superficial, and Shakespeare's intuitions here are altogether deeper than we might think.

I am indebted to the editors of the *Review of English Studies* and the *Modern Language Review* for permission to use the substance of two papers first printed in their journals; to the Cambridge University Press for quotations from Sir Arthur Quiller-Couch's introduction to *The Winter's Tale* in the *Cambridge New Shakespeare* and from Dr. J. Dover Wilson's *Fortunes of Falstaff*; to the Clarendon Press for quotations from Professor E. E. Stoll's "Source and Motive in *Macbeth* and *Othello*" from the *Review of English Studies*; to Messrs. George Harrap & Company Ltd., for quotations from Professor Schücking's *Character Problems in Shakespeare's Plays*: to the Hogarth Press Ltd., for quotations from Dr. Freud's *Collected Papers*; to Messrs. Macmillan & Company Ltd., for quotations from Dr. A. C. Bradley's *Oxford Lectures on Poetry*; to the Oxford University Press for quotations from Robert Bridges's *Collected Essays*; and to Professor E. E. Stoll for quotations from his *Shakespeare Studies*. I hope that my further obligations are made sufficiently clear in the notes, which give the sources of the numerous brief quotations without which an attempt to review contemporary trends in Shakespeare criticism could scarcely be made intelligible. Three friends—Professor F. W. Baxter, Mr. C. J. Horne and Professor F. P. Wilson—have been kind enough to read the book in proof and give what help they could to one already oppressed by the alarming finality of the printing-house. My chief obligation is to Mr. W. A. Cowan, Barr Smith Librarian in the University of Adelaide, whose skilled and friendly assistance surrounded me with the materials for a book far better informed than this.

J.I.M.S.

CONTENTS

Preface

CHAPTER I

INTRODUCTION

He had looked with great Attention on the Scenes of Nature; but his chief Skill was in Human Actions, Passions, and Habits; he was therefore delighted with such Tales as afforded numerous Incidents, and exhibited many Characters, in many Changes of Situation. These Characters are so copiously diversified, and some of them so justly pursued, that his Works may be considered as a Map of Life, a faithful Miniature of human Transactions, and he that has read Shakespear *with Attention, will perhaps find little new in the crouded World.*

Among his other Excellencies it ought to be remarked, because it has hitherto been unnoticed, that his Heroes *are Men, that the Love and Hatred, the Hopes and Fears of his chief Personages are such as are common to other human Beings, and not like those which later Times have exhibited, peculiar to Phantoms that strut upon the Stage.*

It is not perhaps very necessary to enquire whether the Vehicle of so much Delight and Instruction be a Story probable, or unlikely, native, or foreign. Shakespear's *Excellence is not the Fiction of a Tale, but the Representation of Life; and his Reputation is therefore safe, till Human Nature shall be changed.*

SAMUEL JOHNSON (1753)

IF we seek through the many phases of Shakespeare criticism for some cardinal assertion in the truth of which most great names in every century concur we shall arrive, I think, at this: Shakespeare understood the passions and described, or conveyed, their several and conjoined operations with certainty, subtlety and power. It is the opinion of Dryden, the father of our criticism and a dramatist having good cause to discriminate men and dummies; of Johnson, a moralist ceaselessly curious in conduct and the best of Shakespeare's comprehensive critics; of Coleridge of the dispersed and incomparable perceptions; of

Andrew Bradley, whose book is at once so lucid and so profound; and of Sigmund Freud, who distinguished in the plays a regular consonance with the radical workings of the minds of real men and women. Here, one may fairly claim, is the classical line in Shakespeare criticism, and those who would depart from it must show their credentials. Some of these credentials I shall do my best to examine in the present book.

It would be foolish to deny the bracing influence which historical and comparative method has had upon the aesthetic criticism of Shakespeare, or the need for many modifications of our received opinions which recent scholarship has exposed. I am far from thinking that *Shakespearean Tragedy*, for example, can continue to stand without qualification in face of such researches as Professor Elmer Edgar Stoll's. But I believe that the "realists" (as they have come to be called) are mistaken on the whole in the emphasis of their criticism, and that if they do indeed sometimes show that there is less in the plays than Bradley supposes, yet inquiries in quite other fields powerfully suggest that there is more—more, I mean, of that insight into the "obscurer regions of man's being" which Bradley asserts[2] and which the realists are inclined to deny.

I begin by pointing out certain underlying forces which have prompted the dissident critics to take the course they do, and certain characteristic ways in which they set about taking it.

I

In 1772 Mrs. Thrale heard Shakespeare quoted from a pulpit, and found the experience odd.[3] But Shakespeare was already well established there, and if Johnson perplexedly discerned that "he seems to write without any moral purpose" there was Mrs. Elizabeth Griffith intent on "placing his Ethic merits in a more conspicuous point of view," and insisting that "for more than a century and a half, this Author has been the delight of the Ingenious, the text of the Moralist, and the study of the Philosopher." And indeed Johnson's own criticism operated powerfully towards the moralising of Shakespeare, who soon came to be seen as intent to teach. From Mrs. Griffith, who finds in *As You Like It* "a very proper hint given . . . to women, not to deviate from the prescribed rules and decorums of their sex," to Coleridge with his "Shakespeare wished to impress upon us the truth . . .," this conception was steadily developed; and in Germany in the mid-nineteenth century a formidable structure was raised on a basis of moralistic interpretation. The chief stock-in-trade of the dramatist was found to be an array of confident and unsurprising opinions in the field of moral and social philosophy, and the plays were believed framed and the characters articulated to afford an exhibition of these. Such a falsification of the motives and processes of artistic creation eventually filled the Shakespearian theatre with a spurious *dramatis personae*; and a later criticism, struggling after truth amid the confusion thus created, has been tempted to a drastic clearing of the stage.

But another factor has operated in this depreciating of Shakespearian character. Modern realistic and psychological fiction is far more accessible to us to-day than is any poetic drama, and in *Anna Karenina* or *Madame Bovary* we secretly acknowledge a more comprehensible and coherent world than Shakespeare's. Characters in these novels are interpreted for a mode of consciousness and in terms of assumptions and categories which are familiar to us, and except within narrow limits nobody disputes over the psychological impression intended. In Shakespeare criticism, however, all is confusion, and the "characterisation"—say of Hamlet, of Macbeth, of Cleopatra—is a battleground for conflicting and seemingly irreconcilable opinions. Is it not to be concluded that Shakespeare's is an arbitrary world, peopled by phantoms unable to sustain—or even deliberately contrived to elude—psychological analysis, and that Johnson merely talked like Mrs. Griffith or any other bluestocking when he declared that the dramatist's "Heroes are Men"?

Scepticism as to the profundity of Shakespeare, then, first springs from an impulse to prick the bubble of much philosophic and moralising nonsense, and is later reinforced through hasty inference from an observed disparity between Shakespeare's art and that of another age and literary kind. Moreover purely emotional factors are discernible as at play. Shakespeare is a king, and it is not merely Baconians and Oxfordians who would dethrone him if they could. Shakespeare has a court at which the officers multiply as colleges grow; and if our hardihood is inadequate to turning out the monarch we can at least denounce his Lord Chamberlain. The critic inclining to the first of these palace-revolutions hints that Shakespeare is overestimated; the critic inclining to the second declares that the plays have always been misinterpreted. Either the dramatist's excellence is less than has been supposed, or it consists not at all in those particulars which have long won a popular applause, but in others which it has been reserved to the critic to discern. And here I cannot refrain from quoting Johnson, who admirably understood the springs of this matter. He is speaking of the labour of the commentator, but his words apply equally to that of the critic at large; and I may profit from the memory that I have set them on an early page of my book:

> The work is performed, first by railing at the stupidity, negligence, ignorance, and asinine tastelessness of the former editors, and shewing, from all that goes before and all that follows, the inelegance and absurdity of the old reading; then by proposing something, which to superficial readers would seem specious, but which the editor rejects with indignation; then by producing the true reading, with a long paraphrase, and concluding with loud acclamations on the discovery, and a sober wish for the advancement and prosperity of genuine criticism.[4]

2

If the innovator decides to maintain that Shakespeare's achievement, particularly in point of psychological insight, is much exaggerated, and that the classical line in criticism betrays that overestimation of an admired object into which the human mind is frequently betrayed, he will go to work much as we might do in disillusioning a lover by whose transports we are irritated. Here, we might say, is a variety of home truths about all the women we know—and can you continue to believe that Chloe is an exception? Here, says he, is the truth about the aims, standards and circumscriptions of the Elizabethan drama in general—and can you continue to believe in the fantasy-Shakespeare built up by generations of closeted lovers, who have given never an eye to the significant frailties of Kyd and Greene, Marston and Fletcher?

What we have here is a rough-and-ready induction, logically
not very satisfying even to literary folk, and soon therefore the
argument takes more emotive forms. Baffled and disturbed by
the mediocre aesthetic effect of the pearl, the critic first seriously
questions the soundness of his own sensibility; then he thinks of
diving to the oyster-bed. It proves a most ungenial place—like
that

> where Fleet-ditch with disemboguing streams
> Rolls the large tribute of dead dogs to Thames—

and suggests a malodorous mingling of the charnel-house and
the sewer. Here, surely, only the faultiest pearls *could* grow!
Sadly the critic has to admit that the first assertions of his sensibility were not at fault after all. Nevertheless something may be
fished out of the mess, and a clear-eyed reassessment of what is
salvable can only favour "the advancement and prosperity of
genuine criticism."

3

If, however, not Shakespeare himself but his classical critics
be the quarry, the innovator has a more complex task and one
more fully answering to the commentator's as described by
Johnson. He must first show the absurdity of the received
grounds for venerating the dramatist and then go on, after not a
little "indignation," to produce the true foundations upon which
an equal veneration may be confidently built. This is what
Mr. T. S. Eliot has described in another connection as

> revealing for the first time the gospel of some dead sage, which no
> one has understood before; which owing to the backward and con-
> fused state of men's minds has lain unknown to this very moment.

And the revelation will be the more startling if it does not merely
differ from the traditional reading of the gospel but contradicts
it or sets it topsyturvy. Thus if critics have long declared that
Shakespeare's "Heroes are Men" the most complete palace-
revolution will be achieved by asserting that this is what they
are not. And here indeed, surprising as it may appear, is the
central tenet in the bulkiest of the contemporary heresies, which
seems to assure us that the creating of psychologically possible

characters is a constant preoccupation of the Divine Industry
with which it is futile for the dramatist to compete, whereas if he
turns to the creating of psychologically impossible characters
he will at least have the field to himself, and will perhaps successfully construct a sort of Luna Park of the passions in which we
can make holiday for a while, with no thought of the irrelevance
of our artificial surroundings to the realm of sober reality outside.
"All the world's a stage," said Jaques—thereby getting the
matter, like a dozen generations of critics, quite the wrong way
round, for a stage is what all the world is not.

4

But if in all this there is an ambition of critical discovery
somewhat too comprehensive for our confidence, and if in particular we suspect that Shakespearian character is not at this late
date to be written off as drastically as some would urge, it must
yet be admitted that we are to-day conscious of problems which
critics in the classical line have to some extent ignored or obscured.
I do not like to find Bradley spoken of as a "character-monger"
or Coleridge treated with pained indulgence as a neurotic
scribbler in the margins of an art he misunderstood. Nevertheless
I believe both these would have been better critics, and would
have spared lesser men many fumbling efforts, if they had paused
to consider more strictly the nature not of tragedy indeed but of
poetic drama, together with the conception and treatment of
character appropriate to the kind.

The discovery that Shakespeare's drama is not like Ibsen's,
or that as characters Hermia and Helena are only distantly
related to Milly Theale and Kate Croy, does not constitute in
itself a very sufficient illumination of the plays; nor, when we
have grasped that many of the plays are more like fairy tales than
the contents of true-life magazines, and thence infer that the
characters are the more likely to be "unpsychological," are we
treading upon very adequately considered ground. "His
Heroes are Men," says Johnson. ". . . It is not perhaps very
necessary to enquire whether the Vehicle of so much Delight
and Instruction be a Story probable, or unlikely . . ." Is there
any sense in this? Is it possible that rather queer old stories

sometimes afford the poetic dramatist his best field for the scrutiny of the actual hearts and minds of men, rather as the queer world of dreams is the medium of the psychologist's somewhat similar penetrations? Was Shakespeare, having his poetry, better off in this regard with his witches and their cauldron than was Galsworthy with his whisky, syphon, silver cigarette-box and lady's sky-blue velvet reticule? We must consider the special nature of poetic drama and what it entails in fable and character.

5

The late William Archer saw (as Aristotle perhaps did) that children naturally delight in playing shops as realistically as may be, and that this is an element in their education.[5] In just such a sober and instructive mimesis he discerned the true core of drama. But had the little shopkeeper fallen to bellowing his wares and tossing about the biscuits, or his customers to jumping up and dancing on the counter, Archer would have been offended and distressed. Such behaviour, "saltatory" and "cothurnate," destroys the purity of the mimesis; it is a "hysterical exaggeration" to which must be related, in the history of drama proper, much barbarous delight in feelings intensified beyond their occasion and much whipping up of passions beyond the modesty of nature. For Archer dramatic poetry, or drama "in" poetry, belongs with these inordinate children, and only when we have got rid of the poetry do we achieve "the final release of drama from the fetters imposed upon it by a tradition which had its origins in prehistoric tribal life." The poetry, in fact, is a potent impurity, and only after its "sloughing-off" has the stage come into its own and "learnt to hold a plain, unexaggerating, undistorting mirror up to nature." Archer's book is very vulnerable; yet, in seeing the poetry not as so much futile or attractive embellishment but as a radical impurity historically (or prehistorically) conditioned into the kind, it at least witnesses, if inadequately, to the power of the poetry. And this is where we must start.

The poetry is surely not unlike a drug, which will operate upon most people in the theatre and—intermittently at least—upon some outside it. That it is this, and that it sometimes fails of its effect, is the only hypothesis upon which I can account for the following facts. In 1906 Tolstoy wrote an essay upon Shakespeare in which he declared that the dramatist's fame is the consequence of some mass hysteria, and that *King Lear* (the story of which he recapitulates in detail) can "evoke nothing but aversion and weariness" in any man not under hypnotic influence.[6] But, a little less than a hundred years before, we find one out of that small handful of men who might be considered Tolstoy's peers declaring that this play far from being a "weariness" is one to "burn through." No impressions could be more contradictory. Or again, Archer, taking a leaf from Tolstoy's book, gives a detailed account of the action in certain plays by Webster, Ford and Tourneur; and with no more than this account it would be hard to resist the conclusion that these are botched and barbarous fictions. Yet the same plays are highly prized by another authoritative contemporary critic, Mr. T. S. Eliot—and that not (after Charles Lamb's fashion) as the vehicles of stray passages of poetry but as texts for theatrical representation. Just as two men may look through an optical instrument and present each other with contradictory reports of what, for one, has failed to spring into focus, so, it appears, can two men apply themselves to the same play with resulting convictions which bear no correspondence. It is not a matter of taste or judgment differing but of experiences differing. Now both Tolstoy and Archer treat the poetry as an embellishment or concomitant which, for most purposes of dramatic criticism, may be disregarded: and theirs we may call the negative report. But Keats and Mr. Eliot clearly regard the poetry and the drama as inseparable: and their report is positive. We must conclude that the poetry, if operative, enters into and transforms the fable; or rather, and more strictly, that it acts directly and continuously upon the spectator or reader in some way which conditions the whole experience. Tolstoy in a sense was right. The poetry is mildly hypnogenic. We are put into a state which would be inappropriate for the reception of realistic prose drama, but in which such a drama as Shakespeare's can best operate according to its own proper laws.

The most obvious fact about rhythm is its power to induce special emotional states rapidly: it sharpens specific awarenesses while lulling others asleep; it raises or lowers sundry thresholds in the mind. The rhythm is immediately pleasurable, as are the formal elements in every art. And yet this primary aesthetic pleasure seems not, upon reflection, by any means the end of the matter; like pain it is essentially an advertisement; or, again, as pain is a warning so is this pleasure an enticement. Freud has here used a technical word and called the pleasure *eine Verlockungsprämie*,[7] a "fore-pleasure" which induces us to abandon our normal and socially controlled manner of taking experience in favour of ways more satisfying to our deeper selves. When the drug works we are seduced into admitting to our view numerous ulterior significances of human action and human fantasy which the requirements of our culture constrain us normally to obscure; and this momentary glimpse and acknowledgment of life's hidden face has a resolving or composing or releasing effect—the catharsis of Aristotle—of which the sign is a pleasure far greater than that proceeding from mere aesthetic delectation.

Now, if this be true, everything the poetic dramatist contrives, proper to his art, will intuitively take account of the special sort of awareness induced by the poetry, and of the deeper or occult aspects of human action and character from the acknowledgment of which most of the spectator's ultimate pleasure and satisfaction is to arise. The poetic dramatist is thus constructing as for contemplation through some optical instrument which may reveal to a vision failing to adjust itself only distortion and improbability. It is in this way that I would account for the hit-or-miss quality of Shakespeare's art as instanced in the opinions of Keats and Tolstoy on *King Lear*. Poetry, as Bradley said, must be read poetically;[8] and drama, we may add, must be viewed through its right optical medium. If we regard the drama as it were disenchantedly—intellectually and without the co-presence of the emotions designed—it is only by a laborious analysis that we shall account for impressions which we imperfectly remember as having come to us when not disenchanted. Thus in an unpoetical reading motives may often appear confused or inadequate, and Angelo or Leontes may seem not a man but a monster.

The characters, then (but I mean chiefly those major characters with whom the imagination of the dramatist is deeply engaged), have often the superior reality of individuals exposing the deepest springs of their action. But this superior reality is manifested through the medium of situations which are sometimes essentially symbolical; and these may be extravagant or merely fantastic when not interpreted by the quickened imagination, for it is only during the prevalence of a special mode of consciousness, the poetic, that the underlying significance of these situations is perceived. Moreover powerful forces—the mandates of our culture—stand ready here to step in with a sort of censorship when they can. This is why, in Mr. Wilson Knight's phrase, "the memory will always try to reject the imagination."[9]

If it is the medium of poetic drama that permits the use of symbolic or expressionist devices in what remains nevertheless the presentation of true and indeed profound psychological perceptions, it must follow that in the modern neglect of the medium—whether through pedestrian and inadequately imaginative reading, or through the tradition of performing the plays with as much business and spectacle and as little poetry as possible—there must lie a further occasion for depreciating the truth of Shakespearian character. And it is when the poetic drama is no longer with any certainty read poetically that the way is opened for such vagaries of historical criticism as I am to discuss. Communication has become muted or imperfect and the critic senses this. He takes the play from the shelf and cannot discern or decide what is really there. So what, he asks, is *likely* to be there? Criticism holds no more fatal question. The man who poses it walks

> o're perils, on an edge
> More likely to fall in, then to get o're.

I shall try later to introduce the reader to the spectacle of some tumbles of this sort. But first I would examine the work of a critic whose response to the plays is often extremely sensitive but nevertheless seems to stop short at the point where the deeper mechanisms of dramatic illusion come into play. The result, in one able honestly to consult his experience of the texts, is a conviction that they contain a large amount of irrational, extravagant and offensive matter which can be accounted for only by remembering the brutality of the Elizabethan age.

CHAPTER II

FALSTAFF ON BOARS HILL

All great drama tends to concentrate upon character; and, even so, not upon picturing men as they show themselves to the world like figures on a stage—though that is how it must ostensibly show them—but on the hidden man.

HARLEY GRANVILLE-BARKER, *Prefaces to Shakespeare,*
First Series, p. xviii

"SHAKESPEAR'S plays," wrote Mrs. Elizabeth Montagu in her *Essay on the Writings and Genius of Shakespear,* "were to be acted in a paltry tavern, to an unlettered audience, just emerging from barbarity."[10] It was a universal opinion in the eighteenth century. Johnson, although he condemned Mrs. Montagu's book as containing "not one sentence of true criticism," would have agreed with the estimate of fact; "the publick," he says in his Preface, "was gross and dark." Shakespeare's contemporaries in general were thought to have been devoid of taste; "wit," Mrs. Montagu adds, "was unpolished and mirth ill-bred"; and those who frequented the playhouses were, she declares, not barbarous only but "fierce" as well. Moreover this external darkness about Shakespeare was matched by a darkness within: "It has been demonstrated with great ingenuity and candour"—the words are Mrs. Montagu's once more—"that he was destitute of learning." In this judgment on Farmer's essay Johnson again concurred, and Horace Walpole and such scholars as Steevens and Malone were convinced that the extreme exiguity of Shakespeare's education had been proved for good and all. But these considerations were commonly seen as merely vindicating the genius of the dramatist. Dryden had declared him to be "naturally learned"; for Mrs. Montagu he was a "Heaven-born genius" who always succeeded by ignoring the rules and whom no paltry tavern could constrain. The supposed ungenial environment of the Elizabethan playhouse was

useful for the purpose of specific explainings-away; what was
obscure in the plays, or what offended the nicer modern taste,
could be imputed to it. Only Edward Taylor, an old-fashioned
critic who believed that Shakespeare's neglect of rule had been
fatal to him as a tragic writer, attacks in his *Cursory Remarks
on Tragedy* the practice of facile historical extenuation of this
sort.

> Perhaps it will be said, that Shakespear wrote, when learning,
> taste, and manners were pedantic, unrefined and illiberal; that none
> but such motley pieces, as his are, could please the greater part of
> his audience, the illiterate, low-liv'd mechanics; that some of his
> characters were necessitated to speak their language; and that their
> bursts of applause were to be purchased even at the expense of
> decency and common sense.[11]

Thus when the drift of criticism was towards exalting Shakespeare the rudeness of his age and auditory was displayed as a
foil and exploited in apologetics. But with the coming of reaction
the situation changes. The plays are now felt to exist uncertainly
within an envelope of extravagant appreciations and subtilised
interpretations difficult to strip away, and the realistically disposed
critic, looking for an instrument with which to penetrate this,
hits quickly upon the age and the audience. Such, he says in
effect, was the Elizabethan age and such was Shakespeare's
public; inherently improbable therefore the degree of organ-
isation, the refined intention that you claim for this play.

The German writer Gustav Rümelin[12] is a pioneer here, and
significant as having attempted an analysis of Shakespeare's
audience. Most important, he declares, were the young nobles.
They wanted poetry, surprising and abundant action, stories of
amatory intrigue such as occupied their own extensive leisure;
they welcomed extravagance and tolerated improbability and
contradiction; they were uninterested in psychological realism
or in any grave philosophical scrutiny of man and his universe.
From all this emerge certain likelihoods as to what Shakespeare
did in fact put in his plays. Again, there were the groundlings;
for them vulgar comedy had to be provided even in dramas
elevated or tragic in theme; and the fact of this simple obligation
to cater for different palates makes it unlikely—for instance—
that any subtle aesthetic intention controls the juxtaposition of

grave and gay. Shakespeare's plays will be such as a man would write for the barbarians and populace of that age.

Our own time, although no longer so confident of its ability to penetrate the minds and elucidate the tastes of either nobles or groundlings, frequently thinks along Rümelin's lines. The Elizabethan playwright had certainly to reckon with what Thomas Heywood calls "spectators severally addicted," and Shakespeare himself distinguishes among the audience the "judicious" and the "unskilful"—the latter of whom were numerically in a considerable majority and in point of financial consideration an essential factor in the company's calculations. Thus the tastes of the rude and unsophisticated can reasonably be supposed to have weighed with him. That he went far to "purchase" their applause is the ruling idea in Robert Bridges's pioneer essay in "realism": *The Influence of the Audience on Shakespeare's Drama.*[13]

I

Bridges begins his inquiry by proposing to separate from Shakespeare's work the matters that most offend his simple feelings, and to examine and endeavour to account for them. First come bad jokes and foolish verbal triflings; the multitude of these shows Shakespeare's desire to please a part of his audience with whom we have little sympathy, and proves that he did not aim at maintaining all parts of his work at a high level. Next comes obscenity; there is, again, so much of this as to be explicable only on the supposition that Shakespeare was making concession to the most vulgar stratum of his audience, and had acquired a habit of so doing. And Hamlet in speaking of the failure of a play in which "there were no Sallets in the lines" in fact conveys Shakespeare's confession that he had himself deliberately played false to his own artistic ideals for the sake of gratifying his audience—that he had yielded, that is to say, to the audience's demand for obscene jokes. Now this of Shakespeare's admission about the Sallets, Bridges declares, is just the piece of knowledge we require, for it carries the implication that Shakespeare would have met the taste of his audience in other matters also.

It is in the audience then that we may find the key to many

difficulties. Scenes the representation of which is intolerable to us—for instance, the murder of Macduff's child and the blinding of Gloster—we may explain simply in terms of the audience's thick skin, for an audience who are demonstrably coarse and stupid must also be far blunter in feeling than any audience the dramatist would find to-day, and what is horrible to us will be merely pleasantly exciting to them.

And there is something of greater moment which our instinctive judgment condemns: namely the readiness with which offences of the first rank are sometimes overlooked and pardoned. It has been argued that this easy forgiveness was due to Shakespeare's gentleness of mind, and that at least he required repentance before pardon. But the offence of such a man as Proteus or Angelo denotes a vicious disposition, and here offhand repentance is little reassuring. And indeed it is not an ethical idiosyncrasy in Shakespeare that we are confronted with; it is an exploiting of the audience's indifference in such matters to slip past awkward parts of a given story. In this we no longer have Shakespeare merely making concessions to his audience, as in the matters of verbal frippery, obscenity, horrors and defect of manners. Now he is exploiting them. He has seized the initiative, "taking advantage of their stupidity, and admitting inconsistencies or impossible situations for the sake of dramatic effect or convenience, where he knew that the liberty would be well tolerated." The contention is essentially this: that the audience are a drag. Their stupidity is depressive, seductive; it elicits from Shakespeare an astute and effective dramaturgy rather than a poetic drama satisfactory to refined and exigent minds. And at this stage of the debate we have come, Bridges declares, to matters in which the appeal is no longer to the feelings but to the reason. Reason shows us, for example, that Shakespeare, tempted by the obtuseness of his audience, has admitted inconsistencies in the character of Angelo in *Measure for Measure.*

Angelo is introduced to us as a Pharisee rather than a hypocrite; that is to say, we have to conceive him not as an unprincipled man who wears a mask, but as a sincere self-deceiver. And yet when he had been betrothed to Mariana and she lost her dowry he freed himself from proceeding with the marriage by deliberately defaming her character—and this is almost irrecon-

cilable with sincerity of purpose. Nevertheless the postulates of
the main story are clear: not knowing himself, Angelo takes pride
in a virtue insecurely grounded; a strange experience works his
fall; his fall brings self-knowledge and so repentance and salvation. But Shakespeare fails to make this Angelo plausible, fails
to give him a temperament congruous with that sudden outburst
of long-repressed animal instinct which would alone render
accountable a high-principled stoical professor of virtue who is
completely changed in a few hours to a licentious hypocrite
trafficking in crime. And our dissatisfaction is increased by the
manner of Angelo's repentance. His redeeming self-knowledge
began with his temptation, and was complete at his fall: yet this
unmelting man shows no remorse until he is publicly discovered.

> Reminded, as we are at this juncture, of his conduct to Mariana,
> we believe that he has been a solid hypocrite all along; that, having
> no virtue to fall from, he never fell; that the spiritual conflict of his
> "temptation" could not have occurred: and, as there was nothing
> in his first character to respond to the call of crime, so now, in the
> revelation of his second phase, there is—except his demoniacal lust
> for Isabella—nothing left of him to be pardoned and married to
> Mariana.

And yet, says Bridges, *Measure for Measure* belongs to Shakespeare's great period and has master-touches; how strange then
is this blurred outline of Angelo, and how incomprehensible is
the close of the play where Isabella must stand up with the
sinners and patiently endure the exposure and torment of the
theatrical suspense and display which the good Duke has devised
to wind up the drama. And how indefensible here are the
"Sallets" of the worthless profligate Lucio!

In *Measure for Measure*, then, a coherent psychology is
sacrificed to the exigencies of a striking story, pleasing to an
unsophisticated audience. And this *because* of the audience; for
Shakespeare's better judgment would have taken him another
way. And as with *Measure for Measure* so with greater plays;
they are full of "deception," of dodges by which Shakespeare
seeks to obscure the irrational, and therefore intrinsically inferior
and unsatisfying, nature of stories thrust upon him. For here
another constraint edges its way into Bridges's argument: the
audience, if they did not positively demand a play upon this

theme or that, yet virtually dictated the type of story to be dramatised and the outlines of its treatment. And this was disheartening. If Shakespeare had had a more appreciative audience he would have contrived an altogether nicer story for Imogen.

The impressionistic and theatrical technique to which Shakespeare's audience influenced him must be held responsible for another feature of his workmanship. To enrich his picture he will borrow from a story incidents and attitudes without their causes. In *The Merchant of Venice* Antonio's melancholy and his love for Bassanio are examples of this, for in the old story these were explained but in the play are unaccounted for. We must notice, says Bridges, that they are the more interesting for being unaccounted for; and here is one of Shakespeare's deceptions. He sometimes judged conduct to be dramatically more effective when not adequately motived. *The Winter's Tale* may be cited here. In the original story an adequate motive is developed for the jealousy of Leontes, but in Shakespeare's play the jealousy is senseless. Now, the portrayal of this passion in odious nakedness without reason or rein might be proper in low comedy, where its absurdity would be ridiculed away, but in a play of tragic incident and eventual reconciliations it is a scheme of things artistically third-rate. Shakespeare, in fact, is once more exploiting the insensitiveness of his audience to achieve the stagy stuff to which they have subdued him.

And everywhere we have been following Shakespeare through processes that are purposeful and designed. The contradictions which analysis reveals in the plays are not the result of carelessness but of writing skilfully for the audience in an Elizabethan theatre and with an imperfect regard for artistry beyond this. Here is the conclusion of Bridges's essay:

> Shakespeare should not be put into the hands of the young without the warning that the foolish things in his plays were written to please the foolish, the filthy for the filthy, and the brutal for the brutal; and that, if out of veneration for his genius we are led to admire or even tolerate such things, we may be thereby not conforming ourselves to him, but only degrading ourselves to the level of his audience, and learning contamination from those wretched beings who can never be forgiven their share in preventing the greatest poet and dramatist of the world from being the best artist.

2

I do not know whether Bridges was a playgoer, but the responses in his essay seem to be markedly those of the closet. It is in *reading* Shakespeare that he is puzzled and shocked; and when he turns to the theatre it is in search not of a more satisfactory experience but of historical explanations. His method is to find matter that clearly shows Shakespeare complying with coarse and stupid demands; to infer from this a habit of compliance; and to use this habit as a key to the elucidation of anything that bewilders or offends him. But the weakness in this kind of reasoning has been well put by Bradley. "We see," he says of the dramatist, "that he has done something that would please his audience; and we dismiss it as accounted for, forgetting that perhaps it also pleased *him*, and that we have to account for *that*."[14] This is surely the principle to bring to bear upon both Bridges's essay and much criticism of a similar kind. In what follows I shall try to apply it to two or three of the places touched on in the previous section and to suggest that these represent the playwright's relying, consciously or unconsciously, upon the power of poetic drama to open our minds for a time to perceptions normally hidden or obscure. But first it may be worth while noting that the foundation upon which Bridges builds his case can by no means stand without some qualification, and that the argument from obscenity and verbal frippery does not really take us very far.

3

It is very likely that Shakespeare (in this, one suspects, differing from his critic) relished a broad joke. The only anecdote of Shakespeare that we know to have been written down during his lifetime represents him, if not as making a broad joke, certainly as making a joke in a broad situation. And there is a remark traditionally attributed to his father which may be very fairly paraphrased thus: Shakespeare's familiar conversation was sober and decent, but he was not so straitlaced that one would hesitate to tell him an amusing story of an improper kind.[15] This appears one probability; another is that the audience, whether polite or plebeian, liked rather broader jokes than Shakespeare did, and liked more of them, and that in more various places. In the non-Shakespearian drama obscenity often occurs startlingly without keeping, as for example in a dialogue between two kings in the old *History of King Leir*. This may be compared with the final speech in Act I of Shakespeare's play. In the old piece, although it is kings who speak, we scarcely feel obliged to suppose a gag; on the other hand the couplet in Shakespeare's play, although given to a sort of character in whom obscenity was peculiarly licensed, has seldom been taken by commentators as Shakespearian. For this place Shakespeare could not have written these words. We expect, on the whole, a certain quality in Shakespeare's bawdy, and a certain appositeness or propriety of context. But gross allusions of a casual or random sort may be written into a play at any time, and the more we suppose them to be welcomed by the audience the more must we allow for the likelihood of incremental corruption outside the control of the dramatist. And indeed there is evidence of more substantial interpolation. Bridges, in claiming that in this matter Shakespeare shamelessly panders to his audience, makes great play with Lucio in *Measure for Measure*:

> Lucio who, if he amused the audience by his impertinent intrusion half as much as he degrades the already difficult situation, must have been a great success. What better illustration could we have of Hamlet's speech to the players?

Hamlet's speech, it will be recalled, Bridges regards as virtually Shakespeare's "confession" of pandering; and Lucio is brought in to clinch the matter. But it has lately been claimed on bibliographical grounds that the Lucio thus cited is not Shakespeare's.

The regular possibility that this sort of corruption is textual or theatrical corruption is, therefore, not unimportant. Nor must it be taken for granted that where Shakespeare is indeed obscene he is only obscene. In *Romeo and Juliet* there is one complicated impropriety which affords Mr. Pearsall Smith "a learned giggle," and which must have afforded many unlearned groundlings a robuster mirth. But Mr. Granville-Barker has shown how sharply and subtly dramatic is its setting in that whole scene in which Romeo overhears Mercutio's bawdy talk. Indeed Mercutio and the Nurse, both abundant in appropriate bawdy, are, in another recent critic's words, "two pillars which support the whole dramatic structure." Any person of merely salacious mind in Shakespeare's audience who should say "These characters have been put in for *me*" would be altogether misestimating the situation. Mercutio and the Nurse have been put in for Romeo and for Juliet, and their loose talk helps to constitute for us the lovers' passion as what it is.[16]

All this is not to "relieve Shakespeare from the imputation of grossness"—a project of Coleridge's which would require Coleridgean confidence and something more than Coleridgean execution. There is in the plays a plentiful simple bawdy, much of which Shakespeare wrote and some of which he probably did not enjoy writing. The pressure of the age—perhaps particularly of the theatre public—is upon it. But what is significant is the instinct to assimilate this material into the dramatic structure. Portia says things that Imogen would not say. Hamlet with Rosencrantz and Guildenstern is for a moment cheerfully obscene as undergraduates are; soon with Ophelia, and in open audience, he is to be obscene as only a man hard-driven could be. In depicting what was later to be called "the duel of sex" as it exists beneath the surface of polite intercourse, Shakespeare took over and developed a structure of indelicate quibble which is not to modern taste but which has its licensed analogues in every age. In all of this the dramatist rather than the purveyor of Sallets is at work. And we commonise Shakespeare if we are too fastidious to mark the process.

"Bad jokes" and "foolish verbal trifling" constitute Bridges's other primary evidence. And here very similar considerations apply. For some part of what is poorest Shakespeare may not be responsible. Changed verbal habits and deficient information may well have impoverished other parts for us; and it is possible that if Tolstoy, for example, had known more, and a little understood the Tudor mind, he would not so frequently have experienced the "unpleasant feeling, similar to shame" which Shakespeare's unsuccessful witticisms occasioned in him. To this Bridges might rejoin that a serious artist will not willingly burden his work with any considerable load of ephemeral quippery, however pointed it may be in its hour. And yet a serious artist, feeling his way among conventions, may well accept a whole acre of barren ground if he knows that for him there is everywhere fire in the flint. Lear's Fool exemplifies this. His hack-neyed and jejune associations are with a wonderful art made part of the design; strongly accented in the opening or foreground of the action, they serve as a sort of dramatic *repoussoir* for his more effective ultimate placing in the interior recesses of the play's thought. As with obscenity, then, so with jesting. "Foolish verbal trifling" was relished by the audience, and in many forms. There were those who wanted Berowne and "the limit of becoming mirth," those who wanted Feste, and those who wanted Launce—and even Speed. But there is as yet no very certain evidence that such demands were in fact depressive or depraving. Indeed, we may suspect that in supposing an audience potent to cripple Shakespeare the critic merely conditions himself to look at the plays and find the dramatist limping; and when Bridges points to a stumble it will be wisest to see whether we cannot, after all, reply roundly with Ulysses:

> 'Tis he, I ken the manner of his gate,
> He rises on the toe: that spirit of his
> In aspiration lifts him from the earth.

Before going on, then, to ascribe to the influence of a brutal and insensitive audience elements of violence and horror by which we are often repelled in the reading, we should be quite sure that there is no more than gratuitous violence and horror there; that we are not letting the preconception of a depraving audience obscure for us some positive achievement or endeavour of Shakespeare's art when imaginatively received.

The blinding of Gloster, the principal instance of a "realistic horror" enacted on the stage, is, as Bridges suggests, a crucial place here.

$$4^{17}$$

In *King Lear* there is an unusual amount of imagery drawn from vision and the eyes.[18] From the moment when Goneril estimates her love for her father as "deerer than eye-sight" through Lear's invocation of that very eyesight's destruction—

> You nimble Lightnings, dart your blinding flames
> Into her scornfull eyes—

and on to the moment when his own eyes, "not o' th' best,"
make their merciful mistake—

> Do you see this? Looke on her! Looke her lips,
> Looke there, looke there—

the use, the abuse and the cheats of vision are constantly prominent; and this, like Edgar's terrible

> The darke and vitious place where thee he got,
> Cost him his eyes—

prompts us to apprehend a symbolism of sight and blindness
having its culmination in Gloster's tragedy. The leading significance here has been well pointed out by Mr. Granville-Barker:

> The larger dramatic value of a meeting between the mad Lear
> and blind Gloster it is surely hard to overrate. What could better
> point the transcendent issue Shakespeare has developed from the
> two old stories than this encounter of the sensual man robbed of
> his eyes with the wilful man, the light of his mind gone out?[19]

Here is a depth in *King Lear* at which the blinding of Gloster,
whether to be represented or not, has appropriateness in the
fable; and it is perhaps worth distinguishing a further depth at
which this is, if more obscurely, so. There is something un-
mistakably atavic about the play. Like Keats's *Hyperion* it treats
of the procession of the generations and the struggle this in-
volves: "The yonger rises, when the old doth fall." But whereas
Keats would use his myth to interpret philosophical and personal
problems which are essentially modern, Shakespeare drives to
his story's immemorial core in drama and projects the struggle
in that extreme form in which, phylogenetically, it still exists in
the recesses of every human mind. The first anthropologist to
approach *King Lear*—curiously enough, he seems not yet to
have arrived—when he observes how one paternal figure is
deprived of his possessions and wits and another of his eyes,
will certainly aver that these incidents are symbolical as such
things in dreams are symbolical: they veil an unconscious fantasy
of the kind classically expressed in the myth of Uranus and
Cronus. So at this level again—the deeper level at which tragic
drama tends to rehearse archetypal imaginative themes—Gloster's
maiming is implicated with the play, cohering with its primitive

character as a whole and having a distinguishable relationship to yet more savage deprivations in analogous parent-and-child stories.

We may feel, then, that Shakespeare turned to Sidney's story of the blinded Paphlagonian king both of intention and by radical dramatic instinct; and that this distinguishes Gloster's blinding from such virtually gratuitous horrors as Hieronimo's biting out his tongue in *The Spanish Tragedy* and the tearing out of Piero's tongue in *Antonio's Revenge*. As Mr. Edmund Blunden has written of the play:

> The mind of the dramatist is such that wherever we are perplexed we are safe in agreeing with the rustic summing up 'the mystery of things": "It all be done for a purpose"—several purposes.[20]

But this, it may be maintained, goes for nothing, since it is purely and simply the presentation before us that is unbearable and that Bridges would invoke an insensitive audience and a calloused dramatist to explain. Do not the issues, however, interdigitate? Where the governing purpose is artistic the handling will be in the spirit of art. If Gloster's blinding is something other than a mere sensational outcrop upon the play, if it has real meaning in this tragedy of acknowledged genius, then its presentation on the stage is the less likely to be a passing concession to crude appetites and the more likely to be the issue of disinterested aesthetic concern. Having seen both a conscious and an involuntary symbolical purpose expressed in the blinding, can we go on to discover any aesthetic consideration which did in fact prompt Shakespeare to place it directly before his audience? And can we distinguish any specific reason he had for apprehending success from so drastic a show of violence?

The first of these questions is in part answered by a consideration of the dramatic structure. *King Lear* alone among the tragedies has two parallel plots; and this is a device of intensification. Two planes of torment, each with its own tempo, are built into the play. Lear's tragedy is progressive or incremental; and primarily spiritual. Gloster's tragedy is catastrophic, the blow coming in a single shattering frenzy of hate; and it is its awful physical finality that is at first predominant. The artistic purpose is clear enough: "Gloucester is bound, and tortured, physically; and so the mind of Lear is impaled, crucified on the cross-beams

of love and disillusion. . . . The Gloucester theme throughout
reflects and emphasizes and exaggerates all the percurrent qualities
of the Lear theme."[21] Thus the single stroke of Gloster's blinding
had to be set over against, and indeed overgo, the long torment,
the progressive deprivations, of the old king. Somehow, and
even at the play's pitch here in the third Act, the thing had to be
brought sharply home. No mere narration would stand out in
the necessary relief. And so it was the stage or nothing.

This is, in a sense, a negative consideration: Shakespeare took
the course he did because the alternative was ineffective. But
we may, perhaps, add something positive by returning to the
play's imagery and noticing its dominant character as described
by Miss Caroline Spurgeon:

> The intensity of feeling and emotion in *King Lear* and the
> sharpness of its focus are revealed by the fact that in Shakespeare's
> imagination there runs throughout only one overpowering and
> dominating continuous image. . . . In the play we are conscious
> all through of the atmosphere of buffeting, strain and strife, and, at
> moments, of bodily tension to the point of agony . . . of a human
> body in anguished movement, tugged, wrenched, beaten, pierced,
> stung, scourged, dislocated, flayed, gashed, scalded, tortured and
> finally broken on the rack.[22]

The blinding of Gloster represents a sort of crystallising of this
element of physical outrage which the imagery holds so massively
in suspension throughout the play. As a means of intensification
the technique is found elsewhere. What gives the final romances
their peculiarly concentrated or quintessential Shakespearian
quality is partly, as Mr. Wilson Knight has well shown, the
actualising in them of certain of the dominant images of the
earlier plays—that which has been continually suggested to us
through the medium of figurative language being now brought
before us in very fact.[23] In Gloster's ordeal there is something
similar: a spilling over, as it were, of physical outrage from
imagery into action. And in this lay, perhaps, the chief consideration in favour of staging the blinding. By this means
Shakespeare achieves the powerful effect of a suddenly realised
imagery: the oppressive atmosphere of the play here condensing
in a ghastly dew.

Thus if it was indeed the artist who made choice we can a little
follow his calculations—whereas if it was a pandar to base

appetites Shakespeare certainly remains inscrutable enough. Still, the decision was hazardous and he must have been well aware, surely, of the precipice to be skirted, of the exploits of King Cambyses and the Emperor Selimus, of Clois Hoffman's iron crown in the grisly play which Chettle had put forward as a counter-attraction to *Hamlet* only a few years before. May we not fancy him, even, as glimpsing Bridges in his study, or Professor Levin Schücking on his dais,[24] a pile of "the old atrocity plays" beside him as he comes to comment the place? And he had to decide. Here was something in itself crude enough— and were he to employ it there would be many who would never see it as more than that, as other than a scrap from such feasts of horror as Tower Hill afforded. But long habit prompted him not to turn down out of hand even the rudest devices of the popular theatre—for his art, he knew, had abundant power over these.

> In nothing is Shakespeare's greatness more apparent than in his concessions to the requirements of the Elizabethan theatre, concessions made sparingly and with an ill grace by some of his contemporaries, by him offered with both hands, yet transmuted in the giving, so that what might have been a mere connivance in baseness becomes a miracle of expressive art.[25]

This is Walter Raleigh's expression of something that must have been, after all, a familiar fact to Shakespeare himself. Had it any relevance here? Was there any factor in the situation, any overriding condition, that might afford him—here in *King Lear* stretching to its limit the longest tether ever granted poet—a chance of making the blinding of Gloster tolerable and operative on his stage? Far in the future, again, the answer was to be given; and by one of the best of his readers.

On December 20th, 1817, not very long after his twenty-second birthday, John Keats saw Benjamin West's "Death on the Pale Horse"; on the following day he wrote to his brothers:

> It is a wonderful picture, when West's age is considered; But there is nothing to be intense upon; no women one feels mad to kiss, no face swelling into reality.—The excellence of every art is its intensity, capable of making all disagreeables evaporate, from their being in close relationship with Beauty and Truth. Examine "King Lear," and you will find this exemplified throughout; but in this picture we have unpleasantness without any momentous depth of speculation excited, in which to bury its repulsiveness.

Is not this a true perception, which the flicker of immaturity in Keats's response can by no means obscure? In *King Lear* Shakespeare contemplates his theme with intensity, and nowhere more so than in the scene under notice. In Lear's family and in Gloster's the same passions are operative, and the twofold vision of intrafamilial strife is terrible enough. Here the climax comes when Lear's daughters abandon him to the storm and Edmund betrays his own father. But it is Regan who plucks Gloster's beard and Cornwall who blinds him; it is Edmund who gives order for Lear's death. Such horrors broaden the picture we must contemplate and make it more perplexing. For we are aware that these new crimes are prompted by some extension or displacement of the unfilial passions already exhibited to us, and so we obscurely apprehend that in the world about us the whole "mass of publique wrongs, confusde and filde with murder and misdeeds," is but the overflow of evil from where it is most awful. Or we are obscurely aware that social disorder—as the matter might be phrased in scientific terms—has its well-spring in basic antagonisms within the primary biological unit.

The blinding of Gloster, then, is one of the places at which we are required to be widest-eyed, to see

into the core
Of an eternal fierce destruction.

It is, in fact, an eye-opener, and in the issue "a momentous depth of speculation is excited." This sustains something which under other conditions would be repulsive or intolerable. The quality of the poet's contemplation, the height of his argument: these enable him to reach far out into the territory of the hateful and horrible—the μισητόν—and raise what he finds there to the level of the terrible and of his tragedy. What psychological mechanism is responsible may be finally obscure, but the fact is to be verified in many works of art—and nowhere more convincingly, perhaps, than in Goya's series of etchings, "The Disasters of War," or in his two great canvases in the Prado depicting the revolt of the people of Madrid against Murat. These (rather than, as Professor Schücking suggests, Rembrandt's "The Blinding of Samson"[26]) bring us close to what Shakespeare is attempting; and we must feel that the artist has confidence not only in what the intensity of his own contemplation can achieve but in a certain quality

C

of response in the spectator as well. If we can make this response
we shall not be depraved or merely distressed; and the effect upon
us will be very like the effect of tragedy. In Shakespeare's playhouse the corresponding confidence perhaps approached audacity:
audacity such as he displays in many of his great strokes—in
words, for example, put in the mouth of the boy who played
Cleopatra or Lady Macbeth. But it is reasonable to suppose that
he understood his audience and believed that at this juncture
not too many of them would respond with malevolent glee.
And what if some did so? Here there is a final point, to which
we are led by considering the physical conditions of the Elizabethan public playhouse, in which the ruder part of the audience
closely surrounded a stage the spectacle upon which evoked far
stronger suggestions of participation on the part of the spectators
than a modern theatre allows. In these circumstances, and at so
satanic a moment, might not the very laughter and gestures of
the hopelessly unskilful or brutal reinforce rather than mar the
dramatic effect intended for the judicious? It is by just such subtle
casts, surely, that "what might have been a mere connivance in
baseness becomes a miracle of expressive art." And this, while
allowing something to a "realistic" view of the audience's composition, is to maintain that Shakespeare's calculation with regard
to that audience was very different from what Bridges supposes.

There is one condition which might falsify what is here
advanced, namely that the play is (what John Addington Symonds
took it to be) "a stony black despairing depth of voiceless and
inexplicable agony";[27] that it was composed in a mood of overwhelming dejection in which Shakespeare was capable of mis-
using his still splendid powers. But that there is nothing of this
in *King Lear*—which evidences, rather, a careful craft in the
service of a fine spiritual sanity—a noble essay on the play has,
I think, sufficiently shown.[28] In the only versions of the full
story likely to have been known to Shakespeare or his audience
Cordelia is represented as yielding to despair and taking her own
life. This ending, which would be unbearable in his play, Shakespeare rejects; and the text shows him, moreover, going out of
his way to ensure that his audience—even the simpler or less
attentive among them—shall be aware of this departure from the
familiar tale. The point is surely crucial. That Cordelia should
to the last "outfrown false Fortune's frown" elevates the fable

and enlarges the mind of the spectator; and this care of Shakespeare's to lead his audience up is hardly compatible with a willingness to follow some brutal section down.

5

Bridges's argument is a sort of inverted pyramid, and as it develops the audience come to impend over the whole of Shakespeare's art until we are nowhere certain of its integrity. The audience liked Sallets and imbecile gabble and extorted these from Shakespeare; therefore we know the audience to have been stupid. If they were stupid they were insensitive, and therefore they were avid of horror and gross speech, and these too Shakespeare would presumably be willing to give. And soon he would pass from concession to exploitation. The obtuseness of the audience in moral matters, their indifference to just and plausible characterisation if only surprise and sensation were purveyed, seduced Shakespeare into taking a fatally easy road to theatrical effectiveness. For example, Angelo in *Measure for Measure* is pardoned simply because this gave an easy finish and the audience were indifferent to crime.

That *Measure for Measure* is a disconcerting play, with an ending particularly open to censure, has been the predominant opinion since Coleridge, and it is customary to extenuate Mariana's reconciling herself to Angelo, and Isabella's pleading for so wicked a man, by pointing not merely to Shakespeare's audience but to the whole context of the rough old times in which such stories had their origin. Often Shakespeare is constrained to take over tales so barbarous as to be beyond his power to humanise; and where his material was intractable he left it alone.

But we have no evidence that Shakespeare was obliged to take up plots which he believed to be unpromising, and we may be mistaken in supposing that for his drama they were so. Although such stories from the rough old times as that, say, of the patient Griselda may appear to us typical products of an arrogant and sadistic masculine fantasy, and so poor material for a gentle dramatist, they may yet reflect substantial human truth, as folk-material, we believe, is apt to do. *Measure for Measure* is an evidently serious drama which turns—to quote from a fine essay on the play—"from first to last on the problem of punishment and forgiveness"; in ending with repentance, intercession and pardon it ends with "the stuff of Christianity and of the old stories of Christendom."[29] Did Shakespeare really choose to impose this upon a particularly crude yarn the legitimate possibilities of which were merely sensational; and did he in the issue abandon his incongruous aim and retreat upon the moral bluntness of his audience? Or did he discern in the old story a high theme which at the same time held promise of brilliant theatrical success? The question is implicated with that of the credibility of Angelo's dramatic character. If we find Angelo to be a puppet and the audience's lust for queer or lurid conduct the strings, we shall probably estimate the play's ending as so much empty sleight, and the forgiveness as insignificant. If, on the other hand, we see Angelo's fall as real we may believe in his redemption, and so be the readier to approve his pardon and even to see a wise handling of the situation in the rather surprising arrangements of the Duke.

What, then, is the essence of Angelo's case? He is a sincere self-deceiver; sexually he has always believed himself to be cold; and particularly a flaunted sexuality has meant nothing to him. Then like a thunderclap comes overpowering lust for a lady in the habit of a novice, who has presented herself with a plea for the life of her incontinent brother:

> . . . never could the Strumpet
> With all her double vigor, Art and Nature
> Once stir my temper: but this vertuous Maid
> Subdues me quite: Ever till now
> When men were fond, I smild, and wondred how.

It is surely crucial that Angelo's disaster comes as the result of what Bridges calls "a strange experience"—for we may assume that, whatever his duties before receiving the Duke's commission, he had never before had a girl appear from a nunnery to address him on such a theme. In what follows we have something surprising and horrible—this is a grim play—but not out of nature. That Angelo's sudden fetishistic lust is implausible because he does not exhibit, and would even to himself deny the possession of, a "passionate" temperament is an argument resting—as so often with arguments that asperse Shakespearian character—upon somewhat conventional notions of human behaviour; and if the character is to be challenged here it must be on the ground not that it is unrealistic or inconsistent but that it is a study too pathological for representative fiction. We must remember, however, both that Angelo is in no sense the central figure of the play, and that his morbidity is not settled and pervasive, but rather in the nature of an astounding and horrifying overthrow of the normal man.[30] On the other hand if his fall—his sudden sight of the one strange erotic path that he may, that he must, tread—comes as a surprise to himself this does not mean that it is to a preponderantly fine character that it comes. Angelo, with his inhibited sexuality, is not likely to be amiable; and we may feel from the start that he has share in a good many of those vices which the respectable, self-regarding and self-righteous may discreetly indulge: as arrogance, rectitudinousness, cruelty and—in the matter of his betrothal to Mariana—a little sharp practice and self-deception when money affairs go wrong. With all this Angelo has got away successfully—in the eyes of others and substantially in his own eyes. But it does not remotely follow that he is a mere hypocrite dedicated from the first to covert villainy; and he need not be depressed below the possibility of remorse—although when exposure makes first its remote and then its nearer approaches his consciousness of being a lost soul (which is really the good in him) and his desperately self-regardful character (which is part of the bad) combine to drive him on to yet darker crime. In the last act of the play he is like a man fighting his way through a dream, loaded with the awful consciousness of having done irreparable ill: rape and judicial murder are on his hands. And then in a sense there is an awakening from the nightmare, for of the actual crimes first one and then the other is lifted from him as if by "power divine." That which lay unsuspected in his own nature has passed like a cyclone, and nothing has been destroyed except the possibility of his believing that there is anything other than vile about him. That this belongs to a class of saving experiences is an opinion that has been very widely held. Shakespeare, it seems, thought it good enough for the Duke to act on.

6

It is, we find, necessary to recognise that the poetic drama, like myth, is part-based upon an awareness, largely intuitive, of the recesses of human passion and motive. And how vast, how dark, how variously haunted is this Avernus of the mind science begins, somewhat uncertainly, to describe to us.

> Vestibulum ante ipsum primis in faucibus Orci
> luctus et ultrices posuere cubilia Curae.

Of just what Shakespeare brings from beyond this portal, and how, we often can achieve little conceptual grasp; and often therefore the logical and unkindled mind finds difficulties which it labels as faults and attributes to the depravity of Shakespeare's audience or what it wills. But what the intellect finds arbitrary the imagination may accept and respond to, for when we read imaginatively or poetically we share the dramatist's penetration for a while and deep is calling to deep. Leontes's jealousy affords matter worth considering somewhat at large here.

"It would seem . . ." Bridges writes, "that Shakespeare sometimes judged conduct to be dramatically more effective when not adequately motived. In the *Winter's Tale* the jealousy of Leontes is senseless, whereas in the original story an adequate motive is developed." And this is a further instance of Shakespeare's willingness to please his audience by going outside nature for the sake of surprise.

That Leontes's jealousy, or the manner of it, is a fault rather than a beauty is a preponderant opinion. For Mr. Middleton Murry it is "extravagant" and illustrates the fact that in this play the machinery is unworthy of the theme.[31] And Sir Arthur Quiller-Couch, comparing Shakespeare's play with its source in Greene's romance, writes:

> In *Pandosto* (we shall use Shakespeare's names) Leontes' jealousy is made slow and by increase plausible. Shakespeare weakens the plausibility of it as well by ennobling Hermione—after his way with good women—as by huddling up the jealousy in its motion so densely that it strikes us as merely frantic and—which is worse in drama—a piece of impossible improbability. This has always and rightly offended the critics, and we may be forgiven for a secret wish, in reading Act I, Scene 2, to discover some break or gap to

which one might point and argue, for Shakespeare's credit, "Here is evidence of a cut by the stage manager's or some other hand, to shorten the business." But the scene runs connectedly, with no abruptness save in Leontes' behaviour.[32]

It appears to be Quiller-Couch's explanation of Leontes's abrupt frenzy that Shakespeare, conscious that he stood committed to traversing a space of some sixteen years, was necessarily in a hurry to get things going at the start. There have been other explanations: thus Horace Walpole conjectured that it all had something to do with the habits of Henry VIII. Over against these opinions we may set the pertinent comment of a Shakespearian actress, Lady Martin, who cautiously writes: "Such inexplicable outbreaks of jealousy, I have been told, do occasionally occur in real life."[33] Of course Lady Martin may be right and yet Shakespeare's art be in no better case, since mental hospitals are full of patients whose bizarre behaviour is unfit for representation in drama. Leontes's psychology even if real may be held too recondite to be other than that most hopeless of dramatic contrivances, an unconvincing possibility. It is conceivable, however, that this objection ignores a special condition of poetic creation—the fact of the poet's mind being, in a recent critic's words, "flung open to the widest and deepest possible range of unconscious suggestion."[34] If the dramatist can manipulate, and his audience be moved by, feelings of the psychogenesis of which both are unaware, if this is an essential part of the experience of tragedy, then it is open to us to ask whether Shakespeare's audience and properly attuned readers, in his lifetime or now, perhaps acknowledge in such a spectacle as Leontes's jealousy not a theatrically effective trick or brilliant raid across the borders of psychological possibility, but rather a handling, according to the laws of drama, of little-recognised impulses and conflicts within their own minds. This would be but to maintain with classical Shakespeare criticism that his plays are grounded in our humanity; that he preferred men to monsters quite as much as Ben Jonson did, but had a deeper intuition than Jonson of the monster that can lurk in the man.

The protasis of the *Winter's Tale* may be stated as follows.

Leontes, King of Sicilia, was in boyhood the close friend of Polixenes, King of Bohemia. Their "rooted affection" is beautifully described by the latter:

                    We were (faire Queene)
Two Lads, that thought there was no more behind,
But such a day to morrow, as to day,
And to be Boy eternall.
Hermione.   Was not my Lord
The veryer Wag o' th' two?
Polixenes. We were as twyn'd Lambs, that did frisk i' th' Sun,
And bleat the one at th' other: what we chang'd,
Was Innocence, for Innocence: we knew not
The Doctrine of ill-doing, nor dream'd
That any did: Had we pursu'd that life,
And our weake Spirits ne're been higher rear'd
With stronger blood, we should have answer'd Heaven
Boldly, not guilty; the Imposition clear'd,
Hereditarie ours.
Hermione.   By this we gather
You have tript since.
Polixenes.   O my most sacred Lady,
Temptations have since then been borne to's: for
In those unfledg'd dayes, was my Wife a Girle;
Your precious selfe had then not cross'd the eyes
Of my young Play-fellow.

Necessities of state had parted the friends in boyhood and, although there had been a regular correspondence between them, they had not met again until, shortly before the opening of the play, Polixenes came on a visit to Leontes's court. Towards the close of this visit Leontes, upon the strength of what normal observers would regard merely as natural courtesies, falls into a violent suspicion of his friend Polixenes and his blameless wife, Hermione.

              Too hot, too hot:
To mingle friendship farre, is mingling bloods.
I have *Tremor Cordis* on me: my heart daunces,
But not for joy; not joy. This Entertainment
May a free face put on: derive a Libertie
From Heartinesse, from Bountie, fertile Bosome,
And well become the Agent: 't may; I graunt:
But to be padling Palmes, and pinching Fingers,
As now they are, and making practis'd Smiles
As in a Looking-Glasse; and then to sigh, as 'twere
The Mort o' th' Deere: oh, that is entertainment
My Bosome likes not, nor my Browes.

And presently Leontes seeks the death of his best-loved friend—who, he believes, is now plotting against his life and crown.

So much—and in both the passages quoted how matchless the verse!—so much for what Bridges finds "senseless"—and rightly so if interpretation be confined within the limits of a surface psychology. But with Shakespeare, I repeat, such an interpretation will often be inadequate. For in poetic drama (in the words of Mr. T. S. Eliot) characters

> must somehow disclose (not necessarily be aware of) a deeper reality than that of the plane of most of our conscious living; and . . . show their real feelings and volitions, instead of just what, in actual life, they would normally profess or be conscious of. . . . It [poetic drama] must reveal, underneath the vacillating or infirm character, the indomitable unconscious will; and underneath the resolute purpose of the planning animal, the victim of circumstance and the doomed or sanctified being.[35]

It is because of this necessary concern of the poetic drama with unconscious volitions that I now venture to draw from Freud an interpretation of what is going on beneath the surface of Shakespeare's Sicilia. I must ask the reader's forbearance if he finds the vocabulary strange and the conclusion disconcerting; he will at least, I think, be convinced that what one man believes confined to a cheap theatre another man has been perfectly familiar with in a rather expensive sort of consulting-room. Here is Freud:[36]

> The three layers or stages of jealousy may be described as (1) *competitive* or normal, (2) *projected*, and (3) *delusional* jealousy. . . .
>
> The jealousy of the second layer, the *projected*, is derived in both men and women either from their own actual unfaithfulness in real life or from impulses towards it which have succumbed to repression. It is a matter of everyday experience that fidelity, especially that degree of it required in marriage, is only maintained in the face of continual temptation. Anyone who denies this in himself will nevertheless be impelled so strongly in the direction of infidelity that he will be glad enough to make use of an unconscious mechanism as an alleviation. This relief—more, absolution by his conscience—he achieves when he projects his own impulses to infidelity on to the partner to whom he owes faith. This weighty motive can then make use of the material at hand (perception-

material) by which the unconscious impulses of the partner are
likewise betrayed, and the person can justify himself with the
reflection that the other is probably not much better than he is
himself.* . . .

The jealousy of the third layer, the true *delusional* type, is worse.
It also has its origin in repressed impulses towards unfaithfulness
—the object, however, in these cases is of the same sex as the
subject. Delusional jealousy represents an acidulated homosexuality, and rightly takes its position among the classical forms of
paranoia. As an attempt at defence against an unduly strong
homosexual impulse it may, in a man, be described in the formula:
"Indeed *I* do not love him, *she* loves him!" In a delusional case
one will be prepared to find the jealousy arising in all three layers,
never in the third alone.

Freud proceeds to the following illustration:

The first case was that of a youngish man with a fully developed
paranoia of jealousy, the object of which was his impeccably faithful
wife. A stormy period in which the delusion had possessed him
uninterruptedly already lay behind him. . . . The jealousy of the
attack drew its material from his observation of the smallest possible
indications, in which the utterly unconscious coquetry of the wife,
unnoticeable to any other person, had betrayed itself to him. She
had unintentionally touched the man sitting next her with her hand;
she had turned too much towards him, or she had smiled more
pleasantly than when alone with her husband. To all these mani-
festations of her unconscious feelings he paid extraordinary attention, and always knew how to interpret them correctly, so that he
really was always in the right about it, and could justify his jealousy
still more by analytic interpretation. His abnormality really reduced
itself to this, that he watched his wife's unconscious mind much
more closely and then regarded it as far more important than anyone
else would have thought of doing. . . .

Our jealous husband perceives his wife's unfaithfulness instead
of his own; by becoming conscious of hers and magnifying it
enormously he succeeds in keeping unconscious his own. If we
accept his example as typical, we may infer that the enmity which
the persecuted paranoiac sees in others is the reflection of his own
hostile impulses against them. Since we know that with the para-

* Cf. Desdemona's song:
  I called my love false love; but what said he then?
  If I court moe women, you'll couch with moe men.
                                              [*Freud's note.*]

noiac it is precisely the most loved person of his own sex that becomes his persecutor, the question arises where this reversal of affect takes its origin; the answer is not far to seek—the ever-present ambivalence of the feelings provides its source and the unfulfilment of his claim for love strengthens it. This ambivalence thus serves the same purpose for the persecuted paranoiac as jealousy serves for our patient—that of a defence against homosexuality.

It will be seen, then, that Leontes's behaviour may be interpreted as following a typical paranoiac pattern. His jealousy, where it *begins* to be abnormal, is derived from his "own actual unfaithfulness in real life." This is the second or "projected" layer without which the third is never found, and it is interesting that the evidence for it has been provided by a recent editor[37] unconcerned with depth psychology: Camillo, the text hints to us, has been Leontes's assistant in covert immoralities. But it is from the third or "delusional" layer that the catastrophe issues. An early fixation of his affections upon his friend, long dormant, is reawakened in Leontes—though without being brought to conscious focus—by that friend's actual presence for the first time since their "twyn'd" boyhood. An unconscious conflict ensues and the issue is behaviour having as its object the violent repudiation of the newly reactivated homosexual component in his character. In other words, Leontes projects upon his wife the desires he has to repudiate in himself. And in doing this he is taking advantage with typical paranoiac acuteness of something that does in a sense exist, for Hermione's courtesy to Polixenes contains that element of flirtation which society wisely sanctions, since it is a sort of safety-valve and—in Freud's words—"achieves the result on the whole that the desire awakened by the new love-object is gratified by a kind of turning-back to the object already possessed." Only the pathologically jealous person does not recognise this convention of tolerance; "does not believe in any such thing as a halt or a turning-back once the path has been trod, nor that a social 'flirtation' may be a safe-guard against actual infidelity. In the treatment of a jealous person like this one must refrain from disputing with him the material on which he bases his suspicions." This, assuredly, is what was experienced first by Camillo and then by the whole court! And the catastrophic suddenness as well as the obsessional force of Leontes's jealousy, stunning alike to his court and to ourselves as we read, is also described by Freud as typical, as is the sufferer's complete loss of all sense of evidence. Thus the old convention of "the traducer believed," which realist critics, as we shall come to see, have regarded as an arbitrary and primitive device justified only by its usefulness in getting something going, turns out to follow a psychological pattern which is "real" enough, as when the testimony of a servant long known to be unreliable prompts to sudden and phrenetic suspicion of a blameless marriage partner.

It is thus possible to believe that Shakespeare in stripping Greene's story of its superficial realism in point of Leontes's mania is doing something other than sacrificing nature to a cheap effect—which is Bridges's contention. Rather he is penetrating to nature, and once more giving his fable something of the demonic quality of myth or folk-story, which is commonly nearer to the radical workings of the human mind than are later and rationalised versions of the same material. And here indeed may be the clue to a problem which frequently emerges upon any close scrutiny of the plays and their sources: the problem posed by Shakespeare's habit of eliminating or flattening down obvious and superficially adequate motives for tragic action. It is because the audience are unconcerned with motivation, the realists say; and Shakespeare, for example, in making Macbeth do what in life such a man would not do is merely contriving a "steep tragic contrast" by arbitrary means.[38] But it may be that Shakespeare clears away obvious motives for much the same reason as the psychologist: to give us some awareness of motives lying deeper down.

There is no great extravagance in supposing that what is here described is one of the mechanisms of poetic drama. "An imaginative author, steeped in his subject," observes Mr. Granville-Barker, "will sometimes write more wisely than he knows."[39] Nevertheless the supposition raises the difficult question of how Shakespeare himself felt about it all. And just what—at the Mermaid, say, and after a performance of the play —he could have told an inquisitive friend about Leontes we cannot at all guess—just as we cannot guess what Blake could have told about such a lyric as "I saw a chapel all of gold." But at least it seems probable that the dramatist in composition has

access among other depths to that which such a psychology as
Freud's explores; and it is probable that the audience in some
obscure way are brought to share his awareness, and so are not
disconcerted by matters of which a conventional psychology and
an unkindled reader will make little. Such objections as Bridges
brings to the opening of the *Winter's Tale*—the objections of a
mind attuned only to discursive operation—do no more than
scratch the surface of something drawing all its strength from its
own innermost recesses. What can powerfully affect us in the
theatre is, at least occasionally, the perception—coming to us,
maybe, with something of the disguise and displacement charac-
terising related disclosures in dreams—of types of conflict which
consciousness normally declines to acknowledge. Odd as the
conception is to our common thinking, we are obliged by the
evidence to believe that the impact of such works of art as Shakespeare's may be like that of the iceberg, most massive below the
surface. And the sovereign sway exerted over generations of
spectators by tragic heroes possessed of a seemingly uncanny
power to baffle and schismatise rationalising commentary is
perhaps the most striking intimation that this is so. "It seems
indeed of the very essence of Shakespeare's art"—Bridges is
obliged to acknowledge despairingly—"to invent such characters as must give rise to difficulties." Surely this is the confession
of a bankrupt criticism.

7

For Bridges it is only the artist whom the audience corrupted;
Shakespeare remains "the greatest dramatist of the world." But
it is difficult to see why. The core of *Hamlet* is a trick to keep us
guessing, *Macbeth* rests upon a cleverly concealed dishonesty,
Othello is a tissue of improbabilities producing chiefly exaspera-
tion in the cultivated reader—and so on. If we accept Bridges's
interpretation then it is necessary to admit that the dramatist too
has succumbed and that only the poet remains. The audience
in the London playhouses did not permit the production of great
plays, but only of great poetry.

Does something of the genesis of this extravagance lie in the
relation of a twentieth-century artist to a twentieth-century
public? Bridges was a poet whose abilities went unrecognised by

any considerable body of readers in his time, and the supposed exiguity of his output when Poet Laureate even became the theme of jokes in *Punch*. His poetry was admired by his friends, who were for the most part scholars, and he thus stood markedly between the judicious and the unskilful. To the unskilful he ceded nothing and so was the more inclined—it may be—to stress Shakespeare's concessions. At the same time he identified himself with Shakespeare, who, one could believe, had the unskilful as his enemies, and he denounces as "wretched beings" those who will contaminate the divinest poet should he but yield an inch to them. Bridges, a poet incapable of popular appeal or of drawing strength from a common life around him, sees Shakespeare as straitened and degraded by concessions and compromises, where there is, in fact, very often true dramatic insight and energy.

Mr. Robert Graves in *Good-bye to All That* has told how he once opened a shop on Boars Hill, Oxford. Bridges approved and bought his tobacco there. But what if it had been a tavern; what if the Boar's Head itself had miraculously appeared on that Georgian Parnassus? In his essay Bridges speaks warily of Falstaff: Shakespeare surely might have made him as well without such disgusting detail, "in which case he would have been even better"—and it will be wise not to allow him to come "fooling" into a discussion of Shakespeare's art.[40] In this as in much of Bridges's approach one cannot but feel a refinement of a disabling sort which sets him markedly in contrast with another Shakespeare critic who was surely as strict a moralist. Johnson, one may believe, would not have been disconcerted had the Boar's Head appeared one night in Bolt Court. He would have frequented it as he once frequented a London police-court—nor is it easy to believe that he would have remained uniformly silent while his philosophic observations were being made. "No, no, my girl—it won't do." He would have had no difficulty with Doll Tearsheet. And when the repartee was at its most scandalous his would surely have been the final triumph. "Sir, your wife, under the pretence of keeping a bawdy-house, is a receiver of stolen goods." How would not Shakespeare's eye have brightened if, walking the Bankside, he had heard hurled at a foul-mouthed waterman that devastating reply!

Shakespeare's audience as a sheerly commonising force is the nightmare of an ivory tower. Nevertheless the audience are immensely significant for Shakespeare's art. It has become a truism that the plays were not written for the study, and what has been most frequently seen as entailed in this is the licence the playwright thereby gained in small points of logical consistency: here and there a liberty that might safely be taken amid the hurry of the stage. But this of dramaturgical sleight is a minor, as it is often a misleading, matter; and what is really significant is the sort of awareness for which Shakespeare wrote. The awareness of an audience settled in a theatre is not that of a reader over his book. It is substantially a group awareness; there is a merging of consciousnesses; doors are thrown open which even the practised reader can never hope to do more than push slightly ajar. The human mind has been likened in a great simile to the city of Rome—as that city would be if every stage of its development were preserved in strata, the Rome of each succeeding age superincumbent upon the Rome of the last. It seems to be of some such greater and continuing city that we are made free in the theatre, and much is comprehensible there that must begin to perplex us when we emerge. Does this wider citizenship, this driving of shafts, as it were, deep into the mind, constitute the cathartic function of drama; and is the growth of such a science as Freud's, therefore, a function of the atrophy of such great public arts as Shakespeare's?

CHAPTER III

BOTTOM'S DREAM

We are dismayed to find one difficulty after another resolved at the expense of the poet, who is presented to us as a simple-minded artist struggling ineffectually against a convention that was too strong for him.

G. THOMSON, *describing the Aeschylus criticism of Wilamowitz-Möllendorff (The Oresteia,* 1938, vol i, p. 93)

WE have seen how Robert Bridges was troubled by much that appeared to him implausible, extravagant and savage in Shakespeare and how he found the means to cease from troubling in the discovery of a pervasive white-anting of Shakespeare's drama by a brutal audience—the mischief appearing on the surface in the forms of obscenity and foolery and proving on investigation to have undermined virtually the whole fabric. Bridges's argument takes him, it may be, farther than he means to go, and it is to be remarked that his sense of Shakespeare remains classical to the end, so that the dramatist is left out-topping knowledge, at once immensely above his audience and bayed about by them.

Professor Levin Schücking's *Die Charakterprobleme bei Shakespeare,* published in 1919 and translated into English in 1922 as *Character Problems in Shakespeare's Plays,* marks a further stage in the "historical" approach to the dramatist. Shakespeare is now seen as a contented *Volksdramatiker,* a playwright of abundant and superior endowments who is yet not in the least the captive Samson of Bridges's vision. Far from being intolerably straitened by his environment he is comfortably merged in it. His conception of his art marches foursquare with that of his audience and interpreting his plays is largely a matter of exploring their minds. In this proposition Schücking is pioneering territory which many subsequent critics have abundantly colonised—and not always, I judge, with advantage to our understanding of Shakespeare. In this and the succeeding chapter, therefore, I shall endeavour to examine the main arguments that Schücking advances.

I

The aim of Schücking's method, we are told, is to stem a subjective current in the contemplation of Shakespeare. There is in our experience of the plays to-day a subjective element which ought not to be there, and this we are to get rid of by examining "the probable attitude of Shakespeare's contemporaries." They had not the disadvantage of living in the twentieth century, and it is their interpretation, therefore, "which is most probably true."

But—we must at once wonder—is Schücking's premiss here admissible? Did not the very nearness of the Elizabethans to Shakespeare, the approximation of much in their daily life to what was represented on the stage, stand as a perpetual invitation to reverie—to expectations and interpretations in terms of irrelevant personal interests no whit less distorting than the expectations and interpretations in terms of anachronistic attitudes which is charged against us? In achieving an objective appraisal of a work of art our very standing at a remove may help us. Therefore it is conceivably an insecure assumption that what the play meant to this or that Elizabethan is, in mere virtue of that Elizabethan's being Elizabethan, more likely to be "true" than is what it means to me.

And I suspect, moreover, that the assumption, even if justified, is merely sad. For can anything really be done about it? Will not the "probable attitude of Shakespeare's contemporaries" prove on examination something at which it is impossible with any sufficient definition to arrive? The plays exist only as they are re-created in the individual mind and nowhere does there survive an Elizabethan *Hamlet* for which to relinquish my own even were it indisputably profitable to do so. It is true that we know such things as a fragment of Gabriel Harvey's "probable attitude" to *Hamlet*, since he opined that the play had in it what would please the wiser sort.[41] But only those peasants of the Russian steppe who spontaneously took the play for a roaring

D

farce could derive any material assistance from information like this. Had we preserved to us in some wonderful notation a number of Elizabethan experiences of the play it would then be possible to debate whether, in persuading ourselves out of our own experience into these or a conflation of these, we were moving towards what "is most probably true." But it seems unlikely that the historical critic has anything of this sort to offer, anything approximating, even, to a single extended critical notice of the play. It is only too probable that what he would have us accept as a criterion is simply what he conjectures was felt, expected, taken for granted, understood, approved by a synthetic or generic Elizabethan of his own fabrication. And thus, at the best, he will stop short just where the dramatist himself must be supposed to begin. Surely such a historical method is like Bottom's dream: it hath no bottom. Unlike the lady commended by Dr. Johnson, it is not fundamentally sound.

But the test of these immediate misgivings must lie in some examination of the substance of Professor Schücking's book. And to begin with we must consider the argument by which the critic sets out to establish the essentially popular specifications to which Shakespeare, as he believes, closely worked.

2

There is much, the thesis begins, that to us seems difficult or obscure in Shakespeare's art, and conscientious historical research shows that this cannot proceed from Shakespeare's having been an esoteric writer, an individualist working only for a small circle accustomed to subtle disquisition. There was little scope for poetic individuality in those days. Consider, for example, choice of plot. "The demand that the inspiration of the artist's work must be looked for in his own innermost experience was almost unknown in the Elizabethan era," and it was simply keen competition for the favour of the public that dictated the stories used. Moreover the popular theatre for which Shakespeare wrote arose out of an anonymous obscurity, and so was rather like the cinema to-day. Nobody bothered about the authorship of plays, and under such conditions individual freedom, such as is invoked to defend a subtle and recondite Shakespeare, had to yield abso-

lutely to public opinion. Thus Marlowe, who was really on
Faustus's side, was obliged to turn upon his hero, to denigrate
and belittle him and leave him whimpering, cowering and fearful
at the end.

It is true—Schücking's argument goes on—that the situation
was changing in Shakespeare's time. Individual personages
struggled out of the anonymous obscurity of theatrical art, found
patrons, and challenged public opinion. But compared, say,
with Jonson Shakespeare was conciliatory, and his works show
how much importance he attached to following in the path of
popular drama. For special audiences, of course, there might be
special plays: *A Midsummer Night's Dream*, written for presentation before a noble household, is refined throughout. But in
general a general public ruled, and pre-eminently so with Shakespeare. He retained primitive elements which his contemporaries
were rejecting: in *Antony and Cleopatra* the old form of epic
drama with its hostile armies crossing and recrossing the stage;
in *King Lear* remnants of the chivalric play in the set combat,
a survival of the old atrocity plays in the blinding of Gloster,
popular allusive anachronism when Kent calls Oswald "a base
foot-ball player" (this "astonishes us," Schücking says). That
hoary old stage-property, the severed head ("probably known
to the actors by some droll nickname now forgotten"), which
turns up so obstinately in play after play down to *Cymbeline*,
seems almost emblematic of Shakespeare's unwillingness to
relinquish—unlike a number of the rising dramatists of this time
—the close connection with certain blunt and unrefined, but
striking and effective, features of theatrical tradition.

And, above all, there is the clown, clearest case of concession
made to an ignorant mob, "coarse and primitive and calculated
to destroy all illusion." Consider the Porter's speech in *Macbeth*;
"one might as well to-day interrupt the performance by reading
the latest edition of the evening papers to the audience." No
wonder that "the most important dramatists of the time, partly
under Jonson's influence, prefer summarily to abandon all such
traditional methods." Shakespeare, in making a contrary decision, was obviously guided by the wish not to lose all intimate
contact with the masses.

The popular character of Shakespeare's art Schücking thus
takes as established. Why then are Shakespeare's creations,

despite their popular tone, something of a riddle to our intelligence to-day? Precisely because we are inclined to deny that popular tone, to found our interpretations always on the most advanced side of his art and not at all to admit its abundant primitive elements. The conclusion is clear. "An historical understanding of Shakespeare is to be reached only by taking him much more literally than we have been wont to do, his art as more naïve, his methods as frequently far more primitive." And in particular it should be possible "to open out new methods for an historically correct conception of his characters by indicating the limits of realism and primitive art in Shakespeare's technique."

3

What are we to say of these preliminary contentions of the critic? It is undoubtedly true that the conscious purposes, the conventions and the techniques of every artist are in a substantial degree culturally determined, and that all creation must be largely within the framework of a tradition. But the weight of historical evidence such as Schücking brings forward will surely be in inverse proportion to the innovating and transforming power of the dramatist. If we believe that Shakespeare was absolutely without this power then we may be sure that the Porter's speech in *Macbeth* is indeed no happier than a reading from the latest evening paper and that any contrary impression is mere delusion. But if we believe that Shakespeare had a little of that power then—it seems to me—Schücking's approach loses its force entirely. For in this case the Porter *may* represent a crude convention notably transformed, and in deciding the issue there is no possible appeal save to the effect actually produced by the scene. Admit in the whole folio but a single deft exploitation of rude material and we have at once before us here an open question which only sensibility can decide. To approach it thesis in hand will only be to prejudice the issue—and presently we may be combing through Shakespeare's plays and beyond for matter to buttress a position ill-grounded at the start.

It is so, I think, with what Schücking has here said of *Doctor Faustus*. Only to a man pursuing a thesis inadvisedly could come the notion that the end of Marlowe's play represents public opinion overriding an individual conception. The poetry makes nonsense of this view. If we believe Marlowe to have been such and such a man we may, if we care, endeavour to relate this belief to the *fact* of the last scene, but to discount that scene as a sop to an audience is an achievement possible, one would have supposed, only on a basis of mere inattention. Nor is there much persuasiveness in the assertion that because Marlowe was a free-thinker the damnation of Faustus cannot be a reflection of his own innermost feeling.

By this method of criticism is not our direct experience of a play set at the mercy of a preconception? *A Midsummer Night's Dream*—Schücking, pursuing the theme of the influence of the audience, has told us—is refined because written for a cultivated auditory. Very possibly it is so. But can we not imagine ourselves being told, were the supposed theatrical history of the play different, that this hodge-podge of clowns and fairies, this veritable mine of "popular allusive anachronism," could have been called into being only as a result of "keen competition" for the favour of an unsophisticated public?

But for Professor Schücking it is, in particular, Shakespeare's characters that belong to a rude dramaturgy; it is to a better understanding of these that his book offers itself as a "guide." Shakespeare's characters are not like Flaubert's characters; they are rather like those of nursery tales and therefore not to be taken very seriously by grown-up minds. On the basis of this assumption—that the characterisation is largely primitive, and that the primitive is necessarily inadequate and unplausible—Schücking now sets about virtually dispeopling Shakespeare's stage. And in this he is but part of a movement in criticism that has met with considerable success. The position has something gone by default. Even the best Shakespearian theatre recently erected, that of Dr. Wilson Knight, shows occasionally as bleak and empty as a hall hired for poetry-readings by some philosophical society in a provincial town. Are Shakespeare's characters nevertheless still there in the wings, waiting their call?

4[42]

Schücking's first discovery about Shakespeare's characters is this: that the dramatist frequently makes them speak of themselves with an unnatural objectivity, in order that the audience may easily understand their rôles. To this insufficiently dramatic technique Schücking gives the name of direct self-explanation.

In a modern theatre, he says, monologue commonly purports to reflect a realistic psychological process. The character, isolated on the stage, thinks aloud and so admits us to his mind. Elizabethan dramatic technique in this particular, however, is influenced by a close connection between stage and audience. The actor stands in the midst of the spectators and frequently addresses them directly. Schücking regards this as clumsy, crude and likely to be artistically fatal: "The whole dramatic composition and the illusion connected with it may in this manner be absolutely destroyed." And moreover in these circumstances the monologue is something quite other than with us and more primitive; what is offered is simple information on the play, not necessarily to be conceived as part of any authentic mental disposition. It is as if the actor held up his finger to suspend the action, turned to the audience with a "Make no mistake! I am the villain of the piece," and then stepped back into his part. If we misunderstand this we shall feel obliged to explain in some subtle fashion what is merely an arbitrary device for keeping a simple audience on the rails.

And this non-realistic method of giving information, which extends too into the dialogue, is a signpost which will set us on the highway to a better understanding of the dramatist. "The primitiveness and a certain childishness" manifested here "is apparent, less distinctly, perhaps, but recognisable on closer scrutiny, in the whole mechanism of the Shakespearian drama." Direct self-explanation and its implications, therefore, have for Schücking's argument something of the crucial significance that obscenity and verbal trifling have for Bridges's; they afford a preliminary hint that in Shakespeare's drama as a whole "all the details of the technique are more harmless, simple, unsophisticated, than we are inclined to imagine." And this important principle is sufficiently evidenced in *Julius Caesar*.

When Brutus himself declares that it would be an honour to be slain by Brutus we are likely, Schücking says, to view his speech as in bad taste and as a sign of arrogance; nevertheless here, and where Brutus describes himself as "arm'd so strong in honesty," it is far from Shakespeare's intention to suggest a strain of boastfulness; we are merely being reminded of how the dramatist requires us to regard this character. And so with much that is put in the mouth of Caesar: when he announces that he is fearless this is no more than the handiest way of telling the audience that Caesar *is* fearless; even when Caesar reiterates that he is fearless the same consideration continues to apply. Indeed, Caesar is a particularly good example of the way in which failure to understand this simplicity leads to the misinterpreting of a character. For on the main outlines of what is intended—a figure wholly heroic and ideal—we cannot possibly go wrong, *unless* we ignore the principle of direct self-explanation, thereby falling into "a gross misunderstanding of Shakespeare's art-form which characterises all Shakespearian criticism of the last hundred years." If—once more—we interpret in a spirit of psychological realism all that Caesar has to say of himself we shall receive an unsympathetic impression of his character, not designed by Shakespeare. And we are asked to note some of the passages upon which such an unsympathetic impression will be based.

> . . . I feare him not:
> Yet if my name were lyable to feare,
> I do not know the man I should avoyd
> So soone as that spare *Cassius* . . .
> I rather tell thee what is to be fear'd,
> Then what I feare: for alwayes I am *Caesar*.

> Of all the Wonders that I yet have heard,
> It seemes to me most strange that men should feare,
> Seeing that death, a necessary end
> Will come, when it will come.

> . . . Danger knowes full well
> That *Caesar* is more dangerous than he.
> We are two Lyons litter'd in one day,
> And I the elder and more terrible.

I could be well mov'd, if I were as you,
If I could pray to moove, Prayers would moove me:
But I am constant as the Northerne Starre,
Of whose true fixt, and resting quality,
There is no fellow in the Firmament.
The Skies are painted with unnumbred sparkes,
They are all Fire, and every one doth shine:
But, there's but one in all doth hold his place.
So, in the World; 'Tis furnish'd well with Men,
And Men are Flesh and Blood, and apprehensive;
Yet in the number, I do know but One
That unassayleable holds on his Ranke,
Unshak'd of Motion: and that I am he,
Let me a little shew it, even in this:
That I was constant *Cymber* should be banish'd,
And constant do remaine to keep him so. . . .
Hence: Wilt thou lift up Olympus?

In a modern play, Schücking points out, we should suspect that a man who talked so much about his fearlessness had secret doubts as to his own courage, and on the strength of other of these speeches we should call Caesar a boaster and a mono-maniac; but Shakespeare's is not a modern technique, and we must regard the self-characterisation of Caesar as being more naïve dramatically than has hitherto been supposed by the critics. The information which Caesar gives of himself is meant by Shakespeare to correspond exactly with the facts, and there is no intention of charging Caesar with the odium of vanity or vainglory because he says these things. We might as well so charge those figures of primitive conventional art which have scrolls hanging from their mouths describing the moral qualities they represent. And certainly we shall misinterpret Shakespeare if we do not acknowledge that, confusingly and inartistically, he mingles this alien element with the predominant realism of his representation.

So much for Schücking's contention here. Let us examine it.

5

We may well begin by asking whether the confusion and lack of artistry predicated by the critic is something we recognise.

Has it ever formed part of our imaginative experience of the play? If not—if it is merely something excogitated by a commentator in his study—an explanation of the discrepancy may lie in this: that Shakespeare's art holds a swift complexity not readily to be overtaken by a merely pedestrian criticism, and that his dramatic construction, far from being more primitive than we commonly allow, actually has more subtlety than is readily discernible. "The simplicity of *Julius Caesar*," Mr. Wilson Knight says, "is a surface simplicity only. To close analysis it reveals subtleties and complexities which render interpretation difficult." And the speeches objected to by Schücking are valid, I think, upon each of two planes upon which Shakespeare builds: the simple, outward and heroic plane upon which men "show themselves to the world like figures on a stage"; the complex and inward plane along which we are drawn to a knowledge of "the hidden man." There are, in a sense, two plays.

Consider first the simpler play. Plutarch's is a story-book of which the foundation is character strongly and simply conceived, and the people so created leap straight from the page. From the first eight hundred words of the life of Caesar Shakespeare would learn three things, each conveyed through the medium of narrative: Caesar was fearless; he was possessed of a histrionic streak and fond of making speeches; he was ruthless. And what later emerges is equally simple. Caesar had a covetous desire to be called king, and was resisted by Brutus—a man (the first page of the life of Brutus tells us) who had

> framed his manners of life by the rules of vertue and studie of Philosophie, and having imployed his wit, which was gentle and constant, in attempting of great things: me thinkes he was rightly made and framed unto vertue.

To Brutus men referred what was noble in the attempt against Caesar; Brutus was of gentle and fair condition; he bore a noble mind to his country. But his friend and fellow-conspirator, Cassius, was not so well given and conditioned, being often carried away from justice by gain, and suspected of making war more for absolute power than liberty. Brutus believed that Caesar would establish a tyranny hateful and fatal to Rome; he therefore subordinated his personal feelings, joined the conspirators, fought valiantly and died nobly. Cassius fought

valiantly too, for though not so good a man he was full of
Roman virtue. Nor were their adversaries ignoble: Antony took
a big personal risk at the prompting of loyalty and Octavius
spoke with magnanimity of fallen foes.

In all this, and in Plutarch's sense of the effective and defining
incident, the popular dramatist's work is half-done. The outwardness, not in the least "crude" or "primitive," which makes
Julius Caesar so admirable for reading in schools, translates the
simple and heroic quality of the prose narrative. To object here
to Brutus's stern and proud rebuke of Octavius:

> *Octavius.* I was not borne to dye on *Brutus* Sword.
> *Brutus.* O if thou wer't the Noblest of thy Straine,
> Yong-man, thou could'st not dye more honourable—

or to the hard ring, as of bronze upon marble, of Caesar's speeches
already cited, is to bring forward criteria altogether inappropriate
to the imaginative effect at which the dramatist at this level aims;
one might as well take exception to

> I am *Ulysses Laertiades,*
> The fear of all the world for policies,
> For which, my facts as high as heaven resound.

For every age instinctively recognises as a right expression of
μεγαλοψυχία speech of this sort in personages heroically conceived. "I love the name of Honor, more than I feare death."
Here would be an inappropriate and boastful remark for a professor to offer in a seminar-room, but we need scarcely boggle
over it as it is torn from Brutus hard upon the "Flourish, and
Shout" which may mean that Caesar has been crowned. For,
primarily, this is a direct and manly play; and one filled with
straight talk.

But the play exists in depth. And when we achieve insight
into that depth we have not been jostled from a primitive play
into fragments of another and incongruous kind of play, as the
"realist" argument would maintain; rather we have been led,
as a reflective mind before the spectacle of nature may be led, to
view the ambiguities and complexities which perennially lie
behind that simple and idealised pageant of himself which is
native to man. Nor do we find, in this fuller play, that the
speeches of Brutus and Caesar lack propriety.

Shakespeare's Brutus has nobility and great beauty—but Dante would have found that no figure in all the dramas commits a darker crime. How came Brutus to join the conspirators? There is an element of unresolved mystery here, strongly underlined in that groping soliloquy in the orchard upon which so much commentators' ink has been spilt. It is clear that he is concerned for his own disinterestedness. He fumbles after some interpretation of the situation whereby it shall appear to be the whole body of the people who are endangered by tyranny. Yet his final adherence to the plot is insufficiently considered and a matter of obscure emotions at play behind the stoic mask. Is it because he does not acknowledge the lure of the pedestal that he is, for all his nobility, intellectually dishonest? At least there is a great blindness in the deed to which he gives his name and arm. Politically it is futile: committed in the name of sacred equality, it leads directly to a situation in which the populace shout for Brutus as king, Brutus must dominate Cassius, and Antony expounds the subordinate rôle of Lepidus to an Octavius who will eventually leave Antony himself no rôle whatever. Ethically it is indefensible, for "the principles of true politics are but those of morality enlarged," and the only refuge that all these Romans have amid their tooth-and-claw public struggles is in their private loyalties and domestic affections; their only ultimate salvation would have been in working outward from these. Committed thus, Brutus is constrained to defend positions the falseness of which must always be on the fringes of his consciousness. The people whom he harangues as having by Caesar's death escaped the shame of bondage are the same politically untroubled mechanicals who in the first scene were so inexpugnably cheerful beneath the censures of Flavius and Marullus. Cassius, whom he berates for extortion, he has also to reproach for failing to send needed money. Caesar, upon whose death he had agreed because of the corruption that power *might* bring, he comes to persuade himself had been "strucke . . . but for supporting Robbers." Self-deception gathers around him and in the end he is reduced to that spiritually desperate condition distinguished by Mr. T. S. Eliot as cheering oneself up:

> My heart doth joy, that yet in all my life,
> I found no man, but he was true to me.

A Roman thought! But Caesar's last words had been "Et tu, Brute"—and uttering them he had muffled up his face and struggled no more. . . . And so when Brutus tends something to insist on his honour he is no more stepping out of himself to give us a bare notice of Shakespeare's intention at this level than is Antony when he harps ironically on the same endowment. For one who is seemingly a philosopher and a statesman Brutus has acted with too little of reason and self-scrutiny, and too much of precipitancy. But, like Romeo, he "thought all for the best," and his sole buckler is this same honour—his conviction that he is "arm'd so strong in honesty" that the tempests unloosed about him and within him are but idle wind. The conception steals rather often from his thoughts into his speech. But it is a travesty of our experience to declare that unless Shakespeare and direct self-explanation be called in to absolve Brutus from the responsibility of these utterances we are confronted with a character marked by vanity and boastfulness. What is behind this strain in his speeches is the instinct of a man over the threshold of whose awareness a terrible doubt perpetually threatens to lap.[43]

6

For Schücking, as we have seen, Shakespeare's Caesar is simply the great figure of popular tradition, "the Noblest man that ever lived in the Tide of Times." But he is this figure not so much dramatically created as baldly announced by the method of direct self-explanation. Now, on this simple interpretation, why does Shakespeare here manipulate his material as he does? For, first, he modifies Plutarch to give Caesar a more striking nobility, magnanimity; for example, Plutarch's Caesar is prevented from reading Artemidorus's scroll by the press of people around him, whereas Shakespeare's Caesar is disinclined to do so when told that it deals with merely personal matters. Secondly, Shakespeare modifies Plutarch to give Caesar more of infirmity, both bodily and spiritual. Thus Plutarch's notable swimmer becomes the overconfident weakling who has to be rescued by Cassius whom he had challenged. And again, in Plutarch we are told that Calpurnia had not formerly been superstitious but was become so, but in Shakespeare this is transferred to Caesar:

> he is Superstitious growne of late,
> Quite from the maine Opinion he held once.

In these modifications it appears to me that Shakespeare is creating his *two* Caesars, the popular and the deeper Caesar; and is leading the judicious to discern that the overwhelming, immediate and public Caesar is the creation of an inflexible will, is a rigid mask which has proved so potent that its creator himself can scarcely regard it but with awe. Indeed in Plutarch there is a hint for this, since we are told that Caesar's whole life was "an emulation with himself"—so North renders it—"as with another man." And the force of the struggle may be judged by the exhaustion it has brought. Caesar's utterances marvellously carry the impression of one physically fretted to decay, and opposing to the first falterings of the mind an increasingly rigid and absolute assertion of the Caesar idea. As petulance, superstitious dread, vacillating judgment, a lifetime of sternly repressed fears gather for their final assault, he marks them, as Brutus could never do, with all the wary prescience of a great general, and opposes to their threat the inexpugnable *vallum* of a marmorean rhetoric:

> But I am constant as the Northerne Starre.

It is much nearer to boastfulness and vainglory than to direct self-explanation—and yet it is not boastfulness and vainglory either. We are aware, indeed, that an ailing and inwardly faltering man is here vindicating a fiction with sounding words; but we are aware too, as Caesar is, of the power of the fiction. Caesar has created Caesarism and he speaks as the embodiment of this. It is something which cannot but escape the daggers of the conspirators, for it is an idea and mocks their thrusts:

> 'Tis heere.
>> 'Tis heere.
>>> 'Tis gone.
> We do it wrong, being so Majesticall
> To offer it the shew of Violence,
> For it is as the Ayre, invulnerable,
> And our vaine blowes, malicious Mockery.

A grand irony of the play, indeed, lies here. "To think of Caesar as now no more than an empty shell, reverberating hollowly, the life and virtue gone out of him," writes Mr.

Granville-Barker, "must weaken the play a little; for will it be so desperate an enterprise to conspire against such a Caesar?"[44] But in just this consists the tragedy of Brutus. He has killed— and with inglorious ease—an old man, his friend, grown slightly ridiculous in the task of keeping physical and intellectual infirmity at bay. But the spirit at which he thinks to strike has only a deceptive habitation in the man who still speaks so resolutely— with so histrionic a note, indeed—in its accents. The spirit has gone out abroad over the earth, and on the field of Philippi is mighty yet.

7

The Elizabethans were concerned about politics, if only because politics might at any time intimately affect their lives. And politics at Elizabeth's court meant substantially the interplay of a small number of personalities—of personalities often sufficiently enigmatic, the historian now feels. Everyone had a motive for attempting some insight into these—for how many fortunes might turn, say, upon a true understanding of the Earl of Essex!—and this would make for some niceness of observation in the emotional hinterland of public professions. Moreover the Elizabethans, when their education permitted it, delighted in historical parallels, and many of them would be prepared to bring to a Roman history an eye not less penetrating than that which they carried to Whitehall. If we do, therefore, take historical ground there seems no *a priori* case against Shakespeare's having desired to gratify an important section of his audience with a somewhat more delicate analysis of the springs of political action than Plutarch immediately suggests. In short, the "Elizabethan" Shakespeare (Schücking's, I mean) cannot well be brought up in support of a primitivist interpretation of drama treating of the interior mechanisms of statescraft. For here the audience had a strong practical stake in sophistication —far stronger than Coleridge or Andrew Bradley ever had. Why, then, does criticism take the course it sometimes does, contriving to ignore much of the finer light and shade that Shakespeare casts over his picture?

Perhaps there is regularly in the human mind some impulse to reject the artist's or scientist's psychological penetration where this conflicts with the simplifying and idealising formulations of a culture. And Shakespeare here has a discomfiting realism; he disconcerted many romantic critics and set them to reassuring reverie. Thus the Brutus whose personal relationships are so beautiful and whose politics are so insufficient, so fatally of the unexamined life, the Brutus of whom Shakespeare's sombre portrait, sparsely touched by compassion, is so subtle and so fine, was discarded for Swinburne's "very noblest figure of a typical and ideal republican in all the literature of the world."[45] It is an interpretation that meets difficulty as soon as there is a careful scrutiny of the text. But to solve the problem by declaring that theatrical conditions permitted Shakespeare to work only in simple blacks and whites, and that what remains perplexing on this view is simply the consequence of a technique imperfectly dramatic and personative, is to reject in the name of historical "realism" that true realism, that deep and sensitive anatomy of the hidden man, which lies so often behind the outwardness and simplicity of Shakespeare's drama popularly viewed.

8

Schücking extends his argument. Shakespeare's characters frequently describe *each other* with an unnatural objectivity. The bad men, anxious for clarity all round, declare themselves to be bad men when psychological realism requires that they should endeavour to justify themselves; and they declare the good men to be good men when the same psychological realism requires some attempt at denigration. The characters, in fact, afford true pointers to each other not only when they colourably may but also when in doing so they destroy or impair their own credibility. For Shakespeare's technique was inadequate to combine with the overriding value of lucidity the subsidiary value of naturalism. A mature drama is like life; nowhere is there available (as there is in the novel) an extraneous authoritative voice; naturalism therefore demands that the characters appear to us only as filtered through their own or others' minds. But Shakespeare's art could not compass this and—far more than has been recognised—his characters in speaking of each other are mere mouthpieces for passing on his own authoritative statements.

When, Schücking declares, we have appreciated this principle (to which he gives the name of the objective appropriateness of dramatic testimony) we shall have gained "an impression of the primitive and utterly unrealistic devices which Shakespeare allows himself" in his endeavour after an extreme clarity and simplicity. And it follows that "our eyes are therefore opened to perceive a similar state of affairs in other places."

> Above all we observe that, as a rule, the poet is very careful, especially in the exposition, not to mislead us about the behaviour and the character of the hero by the remarks of persons who have a wrong or biased conception of him and who by expressing it might put the spectator on the wrong tack. . . . *The first mention in the drama of things which are important for the action or the characterisation of the central figure must never be allowed in the interest of the characterisation of secondary figures to distort the representation of the facts.*

But—we must ask—is this of Schücking's, with its impressive italics, really so weighty a statement? Indeed, as the exposition of a "primitive and utterly unrealistic device," is it not demonstrably absurd? Every competent playwright will expound distorted views of a character or situation cautiously, and particularly at the beginning of his play. If he there *never* exploits something of the interest attaching to coloured or refracted views we may indeed regard his technique as thin and unenterprising. But is this so with Shakespeare? Schücking, affirming that it is, becomes involved in many pages of awkward comment on a crucial passage in *Macbeth*.

> Glamys thou art, and Cawdor, and shalt be
> What thou art promis'd: yet doe I feare thy Nature,
> It is too full o' th' Milke of humane kindnesse,
> To catch the neerest way. Thou would'st be great,
> Art not without Ambition, but without
> The illnesse should attend it. What thou would'st highly,
> That would'st thou holily: would'st not play false,
> And yet would'st wrongly winne: thou'd'st have, great Glamys,
> That which cryes, Thus thou must doe, if thou have it;
> And that which rather thou do'st feare to doe,
> Then wishest should be undone. High thee hither,
> That I may powre my Spirits in thine Eare,

And chastise with the valour of my Tongue
All that impedes thee from the Golden Round,
Which Fate and Metaphysicall ayde doth seeme
To have thee crown'd withall.

If Shakespeare writes by the book, and with his critic elevates each working rule of the popular theatre into a *Vorschrift* or *Verbot* in defiance of which no grace may be snatched, it is necessary to regard Lady Macbeth's opening speech as an "objective" description of her husband, uncoloured "in the interest of the characterisation" of the "secondary figure" of Lady Macbeth herself. Unfortunately the speech presents some difficulty if read in Schücking's terms. Is it true that Macbeth is "without illnesse," that he would like to attain his ends "holily," that he is "too full o' th' Milke of humane kindnesse"? Confronting these awkward questions Schücking can only answer, "Obviously not." Two explanations alone are possible. Either Lady Macbeth is mistaken or Shakespeare is mistaken. But for Lady Macbeth to be mistaken—to be astray in the reading of her husband's character—violates the principle Schücking is concerned to assert: that of the invariable objective truth aimed at by the dramatist in such a report as this. "Taking into consideration Shakespeare's peculiar technique, we cannot doubt for a moment that he means the character of the hero to be objectively described in the monologue." The error then must be *Shakespeare's*. In declaring that Macbeth is "too full o' th' Milke of humane kindnesse"—Schücking says—"*the poet for a moment misjudges his own creation.*"

Poets, I suppose, may do this. Nevertheless must we not suspect that the critic has here been led astray by dogma and a disinclination to consider the particular circumstances of the case? For surely the speech will be satisfactory if we only admit that the portrayal of Lady Macbeth, and of her relations with her husband, are factors in it; and that a certain distortion of Macbeth's character is entailed in this? On Macbeth himself the speech does indeed throw new and useful light, such as is desirable in an exposition, for we chiefly gather from it that he is not likely to be immediately whole-hearted in villainy and that some spiritual struggle is to be expected in him. But the speech is also charged with certain feelings of Lady Macbeth's which lead her to exaggerate what she pervertedly regards as her husband's

E

insufficiencies, and this renders more striking and terrible our first impression of her. The letter recounting Macbeth's meeting with the witches makes her the more impatient to hurry him into crime—and then upon the exultant " Glamys thou art, and Cawdor . . ." comes the sudden realisation of forces in his nature that may militate against her designs. These she does not review "objectively" but magnifies in passion and scorn. And this should be clear to us. For we already know that Macbeth has murder in his thoughts, and "black and deepe desires"; he has been on the stage declaring these only a matter of seconds before Lady Macbeth's monologue begins. Lady Macbeth, then, when she censures him as having too much of the softness of common humanity and nothing of the ruthlessness ambition requires, reveals herself as a woman so apt for evil that she regards her husband's near-black as an inadequate grey! We shall not be at all surprised when she presently echoes and overgoes his

> Let not Light see my black and deepe desires

with her own

> Come, thick Night,
> And pall thee in the dunnest smoake of Hell. . . .

Lady Macbeth's whole monologue, both before and after the entrance of the messenger with his tremendous news of Duncan's coming, is passionate. And in passionate speech—particularly in passionate upbraiding—not the simplest audience will expect only objective appraisal. The overstating or distorting of a case is natural under such conditions, and Shakespeare follows nature.

CHAPTER IV

PROFESSOR SCHÜCKING'S FATAL CLEOPATRA

LEPIDUS. *What colour is it of?*
ANTONY. *Of its own colour too.*

WE have considered at some length the argument that
Shakespeare's material is incompletely dramatised; that
he fails to make all wholly personative and is often constrained
himself to speak directly through the mouths of his characters.
Now we come to a further "realist" argument. The dramatisa-
tion is not only incomplete but imperfect as well, being notably
lacking in the will to sustain character consistently through the
various progress of a play.

The centre of Professor Schücking's thesis is here. He holds
that the primitive constitution of Shakespeare's art, the limits of
its realism, are constantly displayed in a short-term policy in
matters of dramatic construction. To-day, he maintains, we
expect a play to be far more of a rounded and coherent whole
than Shakespeare's audience did; for them the scenes were the
important units, and if these were satisfactory in themselves they
need be concatenated only loosely together. Thus the dramatist
was free to vary his conception of a character from scene to scene,
and would do so as one effective idea or another beckoned him.

Before passing to the examination of what may be taken as a
test case here we may briefly consider some of Schücking's
preliminary contentions.

I

It is symptomatic of Shakespeare's looseness of construction,
Schücking holds, that he does not always trouble to preserve
throughout his play a harmony between character and expression.
Suddenly, and for a scene or an episode, there will be speech
"out of character." It may be no more than a momentary

rhetorical incongruity, as when Friar Laurence addresses Romeo
with the words

Affliction is enamour'd of thy parts—

an image for the striking out of which—Schücking opines—the
aged friar had left in him too little of the spirit of light-hearted
youth. Or the incongruity may be such as to point us on to
graver reflections on the integrity of Shakespearian character.
And here the principal signposts are Mercutio and Polonius. For
the Queen Mab speech and the advice to Laertes take us thus far
at least: Shakespeare was in isolated places prepared to sacrifice
the self-consistency of his characters to the advantageousness of
putting over matter attractive or impressive in itself.

On Mercutio Schücking writes thus:

> We cannot possibly believe that this character, whom Kreyssig
> rightly calls "the coarsest fellow in the whole company," should
> have so fine an understanding of the wonderful grace and delicacy
> of the Fairy Queen as is shown in this celebrated description. It is
> hard to imagine that he should have been able thus lovingly to
> contemplate and enter into the magical microcosm of animate
> nature. . . . From the lips of a Fairy Queen or an Ariel such
> delicate and dreamlike music of language sounds natural, but we
> refuse to accept it as genuine from the mouth of a bully like
> Mercutio.

How robust the aesthetic raptures of the learned when there
is an axe to grind! We shall not have much confidence in a
judgment which describes Mercutio in this way, misestimates his
delightful gallop of fancy and, failing to note how unerringly it
comes to rest in a bawdy image, misses a simple observation of
character here made: namely, that the gross jests very generally
delighted in by young men are often in the more finely touched
redeemed by a play of wit and fantasy which may very well have
other and purer embodiments as well. And if Mercutio's speech
is thus not so out of character as might conventionally be supposed, neither is it altogether without dramatic function, since it
serves to make interesting and engaging the man for whom
Romeo is to sacrifice himself. But when all this is said something
yet remains to be admitted. Mercutio's Queen Mab speech conveys the strong impression of a set piece, and must always have
done so.

Does Polonius take us further on Schücking's road? His character as a doting and insufficient councillor lies deep in the story's ancestry, and is so obtrusive through the greater part of his appearance in Shakespeare's play that we do look back upon the advice to Laertes as somewhat lacking in dramatic propriety in the light of the whole. Is it, then, as Mr. Granville-Barker says, that Shakespeare changes his mind a little about Polonius?[46] Long ago Corambis-Polonius was an ass. It is not impossible that Kyd, in the earlier dramatic version of the story which we believe Shakespeare to have been following, abandoned this conception in favour of a figure of courtly gravity, and that Shakespeare in the opening of his play followed Kyd but later reverted to the traditional comic portrayal of the part. This would be just the sort of disregard of consistency that Schücking supposes. But is it not at least equally likely that Shakespeare, seeing no advantage in abandoning the comic Polonius, yet modified the picture at first in the interest not of momentary effect but of the general tone of the play? Here are bare boards, and periwig-pated fellows—as in Mr. Wopsle's *Hamlet* late-risen from the people[47]—preparing to stride across them. Dignity, a heroic tone even, must be given to the representation as it begins to move us. At the start at least Polonius had better a little personify the councils of princes. We may, if we choose, consider that we here touch one of the "limits of Shakespeare's realism." But it is dramatic artistry, not naïveté, that is at work, and in the interest of this it seems of small account that Polonius must suspend his dotage for a scene, and then decline into the vale of years with something of the inexplicable speed of many Shakespearian journeys.

2

But we are directed next to whole episodes which, although they do not noticeably violate psychological probability, are yet artistically crude because irrelevant to the action of the play. Shakespeare, it is maintained, seems willing to thrust in these episodes for the sake of whatever isolated interest he can give them, and this shows how ready he is to work simply in terms of a succession of striking scenes. Rümelin has remarked of theatrical effect "how little it depends on the systematic arrangement and harmony of the whole and how much on the attractive and thrilling nature of the single parts"; and this opinion Schücking takes up and greatly magnifies. Elizabethan plays "might actually be nothing but *bundles of scenes*," and Shakespeare took full advantage of such licence for "the insertion of much inartistic matter consisting largely of anachronisms and topical allusions." After citing two instances of this Schücking goes on:

> In these we clearly see to what extent the Shakespearian drama can occasionally dispense with internal coherence. But we must not suppose that we are dealing here with exceptional cases. In reality this practice is nothing but a symptom of Shakespeare's supreme interest in the single scene, which all his knowledge of dramatic art cannot induce him to subordinate to the interest of the whole to the extent that is demanded by a later period.

It will be worth while briefly to examine the two instances upon which Schücking rests his demonstration of Shakespeare's proneness to isolated and inartistic episode exploited without regard to a whole. They are Hamlet's concern over the distress and worries of the city tragedians and the scene in *Macbeth* which tells of King Edward the Confessor's supernatural power of healing. This latter—the very short episode descriptive of the King's Evil—is declared to be "thrust into the play apparently without any artistic scruples," and for this there is an "obvious reason" in Shakespeare's anxiety to please King James, who fancied that Edward's miraculous power had descended to him. The obvious reason is unquestionably operative; nevertheless it is a mistake to rest content with it. Apply to the incident that sort of test of relevance which would be appropriate to what publishers call action-fiction and it undoubtedly stands out as pointless and isolated. But discern as master-themes in *Macbeth* the ideas of Order, Kingship, Evil and Grace, and it will be hard indeed to see in this passage, so deliberately placed between Malcolm's suspicious fencing with Macduff and Ross's arrival with news of the state of Scotland, any "symptom of Shakespeare's supreme interest in the single scene."[48] Shakespeare simultaneously flatters James and pursues his imaginative design. The dexterity may be disconcerting but it is scarcely crude or the work of one content to leave dramatic standards as he finds them. What, then, of Hamlet and the players?

Let it be admitted at once that in *Hamlet* the discussion of what may clearly be read as London theatrical conditions incorporates an appeal to a somewhat undisciplined taste; the passage pleased an audience which had of late developed a fancy for fleeting allusions to current theatrical affairs. But let Bradley's caution also be remembered: the passage may have pleased Shakespeare —and an exigent Shakespeare—too. Few critics, I suppose, would deny that to Hamlet, as to no other tragic hero, Shakespeare is concerned to give an envelope of markedly contemporary feeling, displaying him as a cultivated Renaissance gentleman, one in whom melancholy is at war with keen and catholic intellectual interests. Could anything more economically convey this impression than these brief, well-informed questions on the theatrical companies, and the excellent talk on plays and players?

But we are told that Shakespeare regarded chiefly the effectiveness of the individual scene and was careless of any more comprehensive unity. From this we are to infer that he would be careless too of sustained characterisation. And upon this, again, we are to hunt about and find the characters indeed protean. But in the very place in which chief toll is here levied Hamlet has something to say on "an excellent Play" and the first thing he remarks is its being "well digested in the Scoenes"—a judgment which can refer only to the just disposition of the parts in relation to the whole. Concerned as he is to argue from Shakespeare's standards and intentions, ought Professor Schücking to have passed over this piece of evidence? And it is noteworthy that Tolstoy, who goes so much further than Schücking in many places, excepts from his condemnation "the masterly development of the scenes, which constitutes Shakespeare's speciality."

So far, our tentative conclusion might be something like this: that Shakespeare's compliance with the low standards of coherence and consistency undoubtedly prevalent in the theatre for which he wrote is something that it is unsafe in any specific instance to assert without close scrutiny, for it was second nature with him to make the simplicities of his craft tell in subtle ways too. Nevertheless on all this we should keep an open mind until we have seen Schücking deploy some of his heavier forces on the field.

3

Shakespeare's plays contain a number of discrepancies and loose ends. Othello is momentarily dowered with a brother in whose existence we can feel little confidence; Antonio in *The Tempest* is described as having a son saved from the wreck, but the son never appears; Prospero in the same play declares that graves have opened at his command, although the island where this has happened has always been uninhabited; Horatio claims to remember King Hamlet's expression as he smote the sledded Polacks, an event which must have occurred when Horatio was in his nursery. The explanation of such discrepancies, Schücking reasonably declares, is that Shakespeare's art, because it lived in the spoken word, paid little attention to an exact correspondence of all the details. And here is evidence of a method of work likely to give rise to contradictions in the portrayal of character. Shakespeare, thinking in terms of the effective part rather than the coherent whole, is betrayed into "different conceptions of the same character in different scenes." And thus from Othello's brother we proceed to Antony's mistress. Cleopatra is a "remarkable and disturbing" instance of inconsistency of this sort.

But this, after all, is rather what Antony found! And although nothing calls more sharply for accurate and sensitive psychology than the portrayal of a woman's mutability, so that Shakespeare may indeed have failed in the task, yet the fact of the historical Cleopatra's being the acknowledged prototype of all those with power to keep their fellow mortals guessing makes the proposal to find here the key-instance of inconsistency in Shakespearian character-portrayal an extremely ticklish business. Why, then, does Schücking choose Cleopatra? Partly, it seems, because she is in a play which he judges particularly *likely* to harbour inconsistent characters. In *Antony and Cleopatra*, "the older form of the primitive epic drama comes to light again"; it is an exceptionally step-by-step play, a congeries of isolated and self-sufficient scenes.

I do not know that there is very much in this; it is a view dating from the days when in a presentation of *Antony and Cleopatra* the curtain would come bumping or swishing down forty-two times. At least we may oppose to it the verdict of the theatre in its most authoritative contemporary embodiment. "There is," writes Mr. Granville-Barker, "no juncture where the play's acting will be made more effective by a pause. On the contrary, each scene has an effective relation to the next, which a pause between them will weaken or destroy."[49] In fact, there is more than one way of ordering scenes, and when Schücking declares that a scene is "isolated" he may merely mean that it is not linked to its neighbours in the particular way in which, he judges, it *ought* to be linked: in terms of simple narrative development. In *Antony and Cleopatra*, therefore, the extent to which Shakespeare achieves a play "well-digested in the scenes" is not to be estimated in terms of the play's divergence from other plays of admitted formal strength. There can be more than one sort of formal strength. It is pointless to bring the canons of Poussin to the compositions of Cézanne.

But Schücking brings forward a second preliminary contention. In *Antony and Cleopatra*, besides "dramatic formlessness, there are to be clearly discerned signs of a rapid and careless workmanship. In numerous places it becomes imperative to look up the corresponding passage in Plutarch in order to understand what is meant." (For instance, Cleopatra and her attendants cry "To the monument," when we have been told nothing about it.) And Schücking takes for granted the probability of correla.ion between such slips and "carelessness" of the most fundamental sort. The dramatist who, turning to his source, misses the precise point of an omen through picking it from the gloss and not from the text; who fails to carry over from Plutarch those details which would tell us that Antony's invitation to Caesar to whip his freedman Hipparchus is a malicious joke; who makes Pompey say, "Oh *Anthony*, you have my Father's house," and leaves the remark wholly mysterious: such a dramatist is the likelier to give us a protean Cleopatra.

We may ask, however, if carelessness of the "To the monument" order is really likely to march with carelessness in the fundamental conception of a principal character. In a work pervasively slipshod and uninterested it would be so. But is *Antony and Cleopatra* to be described in such terms?

ACTUS PRIMUS. SCOENA PRIMA

Enter DEMETRIUS *and* PHILO

Philo. Nay, but this dotage of our Generals
Ore-flowes the measure: those his goodly eyes
That o're the Files and Musters of the Warre,

Have glow'd like plated Mars: now bend, now turne
The Office and Devotion of their view
Upon a Tawny Front. His Captaines heart,
Which in the scuffles of great Fights hath burst
The Buckles on his brest, reneages all temper,
And is become the Bellowes and the Fan
To coole a Gypsies Lust.

Flourish. Enter ANTHONY, CLEOPATRA, *her Ladies, the Traine, with Eunuchs fanning her.*

Looke where they come:
Take but good note, and you shall see in him
The triple Pillar of the world transform'd
Into a Strumpets Foole. Behold and see.
Cleopatra. If it be Love indeed, tell me how much.

Philo's opening speech is very wonderful; Cleopatra's first line, in what it gives the player, is, I suppose, more wonderful still. Do we not know at once that Shakespeare is here at a high level of creativeness, unfettered and unstrained? Other plays may turn out to be profounder, but none takes from the start so confident a grasp of so large matter, or ventures to open at such a pitch. What then in *this* context, a context of large and certain craft, of easy and delighted power, are fugitive signs of "careless workmanship" likely to signify? Pretty well the reverse, possibly, of what Schücking supposes. The neglect of minor consistencies and correspondences is simply a function of concentration upon a whole which has been apprehended with unusual urgency in that mysterious world, beyond common consciousness, in which the artist's creations live.

4

The "bundle of scenes" aspect of *Antony and Cleopatra*, then, may be more apparent than real; and there is little force in the suggestion that the play in evidencing small faults is the more likely to harbour great. So what, if we set aside preconceptions based on either the construction of the play or the supposed tendencies of Shakespearian character in general, is the actual case for a non-integrated Cleopatra, a Cleopatra who is a mere sum or tale of theatrical conveniences? "Different Conceptions

of the Same Character in Different Scenes" is Schücking's head-
ing here. How is it substantiated?

The contention runs something like this. Cleopatra in popular
tradition was the type of the great courtesan, and an audience
would therefore bring to a play about her certain expectations
which Shakespeare would be concerned to fulfil—the more so as
Antony and Cleopatra was written during a vogue for dramatic
presentations of prostitution and bawdry. At the start therefore
Shakespeare would be inclined to neglect those aspects of
Plutarch's Cleopatra—her culture, statecraft, power to hold
Antony by entering into his interests—which might conflict
with this simple conception. But in thus following his usual
short-term policy Shakespeare was laying up trouble for himself
ahead. For he was telling Plutarch's story, and his Cleopatra
must be Plutarch's Cleopatra in the end, and this would entail
adopting a new conception of the character somewhere in the
progress of the play.

At the start, then, Schücking declares, Shakespeare makes his
Cleopatra a creature living entirely between sensuality and list-
lessness, without refinement, vulgar, a mere shrew devoid of
self-control, treating her servants as a servant-become-mistress
would do, acting in moments of passion like a hysterical harlot.
She exercises a harlot's trade. She takes a vulgar pride in former
lovers and her behaviour towards Antony is dominated by
calculation. Her love, if it exists, is selfish and superficial, so that
she is incapable of regarding anything from her lover's point of
view. We should not be inclined to prophesy that such a love
would be of long duration; and altogether it is "rather curious
that a number of critics grow quite enthusiastic" about Cleopatra
as she is exhibited in the early part of the play. Sounder—we
must believe—are those commentators who can be dug out of
the *Variorum* and marshalled in a condemnatory camp: Hallam,
who speaks of "this character being not one that can please";
Hartley Coleridge, who warns us (much in the tones of his
father, when addressing Nonconformist lecture-audiences) that
"the interest, though not dangerous, is not perfectly agreeable";
Corson, who points out that "in all the scenes in which Cleopatra
appears, she is not a very fascinating creature"; or Skottowe, who
declares that "Shakespeare has not been successful in conveying
an idea of the elegance of Cleopatra's mind. Neither her manners,

thoughts, nor language, impress us with a conviction of her possessing those accomplishments which Plutarch ascribes to her." And all this is deliberate on the dramatist's part. For Schücking sternly rejects the suggestion that "Shakespeare has merely omitted, by an oversight, to insert a scene in which Cleopatra's grace, wit, or any other of her attractions were actually shown." Shakespeare's early view of Cleopatra is simply that of Enobarbus when he designates her briefly and contemptuously as Mark Antony's "Egyptian dish."

Unfortunately, Schücking continues, Shakespeare was not in a position to leave ill alone. And instead of preserving his Cleopatra "intelligent, passionate, astute, heartless, essentially vulgar, and profoundly immoral," he presently develops an "astonishing contradiction"; Cleopatra becomes "a thoughtful and motherly woman"; she is like Desdemona, like Juliet, like the wife of Brutus; she takes on calm, resolution, an iron strength, something sublime. And "this woman, who now is inwardly as well as outwardly a queen, has but little in common with the harlot of the first part. . . . Consistent development of the character Shakespeare has put before us in the first part would require that she should endeavour to extricate herself from the fate that threatens Antony. But she does not make any attempt to do so." What we are given in the latter part of the play, in fact, is "a complete and separate individual." Nor can there be any question of "development" (such as we find in "a proper drama of character development like *The Honest Whore*"). For "the Cleopatra whom we see in the time of Antony's good fortune gives us no indication of that moral substructure on which alone the fortitude she shows in adversity can rest." How can we accept the achieving of "what's brave, what's noble" by a woman for long demonstrably without magnanimity? It is all very well for Shakespeare, becoming aware of the hopelessly dual nature of his creation, to thrust in some hint of development:

> I am marble-constant, *now* the fleeting moon
> No planet is of mine.

This does not get away from the fact that the Cleopatra of the first part has been designed without regard to the course which history, enshrined in Plutarch, demands that the action should finally take. Of Lady Macbeth's weakness we are at least given

hints in the earlier part of the play. But of Cleopatra's strength
we are given no hint. And so the "two physiognomies" remain
"irreconcilable." A woman behaving as Cleopatra does early in
the play would not, in fact, behave as Cleopatra does later in the
play. Common observation yields some power of prediction in
the field of human behaviour, and in the light of this Cleopatra's
vagaries are seen to be altogether out of nature.

But are they indeed so? And is Professor Schücking right?

5

Life holds far less of the predictable than we find it convenient
to assert. And those who would require more "consistency" of
Cleopatra are, I would suggest, making the same sort of demand
upon a dramatic personage as society or a culture makes upon
the individual—the demand that the individual should conform
to his definition, that he should, even amid disruptive experiences,
vindicate the fixity and intelligibility of his character against the
fluid and mysterious personality that lies below, that he should
do this in the interest of the general lucidity of things.

For on what sort of common observation, it must be asked,
does Schücking rely? Probably few people who venture an
opinion on Cleopatra have much acquaintance with dissipated
queens, with courtesans, or even with harlots. Few have watched
a complex woman flee from a sea-battle or reconcile herself with
a lover after such a flight or later draw him up, dying, into a
beleaguered monument. The number of people who have witnessed a royal suicide must be extremely small. Thus in the
judging of Cleopatra's verisimilitude the appeal is to observation
through a series of inferences only. Or the appeal is to "human
nature." Now by this touchstone we commonly suppose ourselves to mean a body of knowledge, built up from disinterested
observation of the behaviour of uninhibited human beings. But
this is inaccurate. The concept "human nature" is shaped
primarily not by such observations (which are, in fact, very little
available to us) but by the system of proprieties operative in the
culture to which we belong. "Much of what we ascribe to
human nature"—as the American anthropologist Franz Boas
puts it—"is no more than a reaction to the restraints put upon us

by our civilization."⁵⁰ It follows from this that when we assess the "consistency" of an imaginary individual we are likely to be doing so, far more than we are aware, in terms of the substantially arbitrary assertions of our own particular society. And cultures differ widely in their conceptions of human nature and the verisimilar: behaviour which in the opinion of those within a culture is perfectly consistent may appear wildly inconsistent to an observer from without. For example, most North American Indians would see in the behaviour-sequence *vision-exaltation* consistent conduct, something true to human nature, since visions bring a coveted supernatural power. But a wanderer from the south-west Pueblos would see in this a startlingly inconsistent behaviour-sequence, since he regards a vision as a sign of death, and *vision-dejection* therefore as the association that human nature requires. Or again, a visitor from the mountain-dwelling Arapesh of New Guinea to the river-dwelling Mundugumor would find bafflingly inconsistent the conduct of a man who first got his wife with child and then left her the major share in looking after the baby. And a visitor from the river-dwelling Mundugumor to the lake-dwelling Tchambuli would judge as even more inconsistent men who first bought their wives (as men should do) and then handed them the control of the whole economic and practical life of the community (an act of inconceivable abnegation). A man who does this must present to the good Mundugumor precisely what Cleopatra presents to Schücking: "two physiognomies which are irreconcilable."

What is held native to and predictable of a woman of wide erotic experience will vary as between communities with varying social ideologies. "Human nature" will issue substantially different decrees to the *dicteriades* and the *hetaerae* of Athens, the *hierodouloi* of Corinth, the *meretriculae* of Rome and the puzzling ladies of Flaubert's Paris—while on the Oder, too, there will be ineluctable laws. And to a considerable extent the definition will be obeyed and the individual will conform. Sometimes, of course, innate temperament, a deeper individuality, will declare itself in conduct altogether violating the particular system of expectations sanctioned by the community: nevertheless these expectations will continue to be asserted even in the face of evidence by which they are demonstrably falsified. There have been savages who denied the existence of the missionaries' gardens in which they laboured, since the missionaries had declined to use the magic from which alone a garden could consistently spring. The vegetation had acted out of character; it had failed to conform to its definition; and so it was *not there*. Is not a somewhat similar mechanism at work in those who would deny the existence —for that is what it comes to—of Shakespeare's Cleopatra?

6

And here it is perhaps possible to make a more general statement. In life, the concept of "character" may be likened in part to a choreographic score, which disciplines and concentrates the instinctive movements of the dancer, defining the steps which he may properly take. And the individual yields himself to the dance, to the pattern which the social purpose imposes. The movements become instinctive, seemingly of the essence of the man. But this to which he gives himself is not nature; it is a convention, a mask; and behind it or below is the sheer personality, intact and mysterious. And sometimes the flame burns through, the dancer breaks from the pattern, the player renounces, transforms, enriches his part, the social man rebels from his determined road and vindicates the lurking deviant in us all. And, at this, tragedy or the seed of tragedy is achieved. The spectacle is no longer ordered and Apollonian only, but inordinate and Dionysian as well. It is Apollonian art, however, that is invariably demanded by all that is conservative and centripetal in a culture. Following its ethos we require first of a spectacle or a character that it be socially intelligible—accountable in terms of the human situation and human nature as our culture declares these to be. Hence the arbitrariness that much literature imposes upon life, the determination to reduce the variousness of human behaviour to a manageable number of paths, to certain accepted rôles. Hence too in literature of some sophistication the demand that conduct should, upon analysis, appear to be culturally determined; that the individual should be displayed developing predictably under the interplay of known social forces, should be imprisoned indeed within the system these forces compose, should be prompted from no depths uncontrolled by them, should win nothing from a void. But from this let us return to Cleopatra.

7

In our society a sensually uncontrolled woman is potentially more disruptive than a sensually uncontrolled man, and as a consequence different behaviour-patterns and systems of expectation are built up for the two sexes. A man may have many mistresses and nobody will think to say he "exercises a trade" simply on the strength of his exploiting his sexual attractiveness to gain sexual gratification (which is demonstrably all, we must note, that Cleopatra can be charged with doing). Nor—unless he is wholly a debauchee—is such a man judged markedly incapable of fidelity or less likely than another to show "fortitude" when adversity comes. But a woman with many lovers it is expedient to regard as in different case; more odium attaches to her change of troth, any ultimate fidelity is supposed to be beyond her reach, and—since she is economically the dependent partner—the play of her sensuality is quickly felt to be shot with mercenary considerations.

It is to something like this social construct, then, that Schücking gives the name "harlot," and to which, like Enobarbus, he bluffly approximates the living Cleopatra. Looking through the spectacles of an institutionalised psychology, he sees her—as the quick comedians were to do—in the posture of a whore, and therefore with only a whore's progress before her. But this is to decline comparing her with women as they live their life in the world—perpetually surprising because their underlying nature leads them now to fulfil and now to betray the traditional expectations formulated by a culture; rather it is drastically to simplify and categorise her in terms of these formulations; it is to apply a formal mode of regarding character derived less from nature than from fictions that have come to be felt as true merely because they are socially expedient, and which have consequently come to be embodied in common literary convention. Bradley distinguishes the whole process in a sentence:

> Shakespeare's famous characters . . . in passing from the mind of their creator into other minds, suffer change; they tend to lose their harmony through the disproportionate attention bestowed on some one feature, or to lose their uniqueness by being conventionalised into types already familiar.[51]

And Schücking simply does this twice in regard to the same character. At the beginning of the play he conventionalises Cleopatra into a harlot, thrusting her, as it were, into one brothel along with Aretino's Nanna and Pippa. At the end of the play, when it has become evident that this will no longer do, he abruptly introduces her to Desdemona, Juliet and Brutus's Portia; finds her to be a "thoughtful and motherly woman"; and finally reconventionalises her as a "Thusnelda in chains." And behind Thusnelda still is the harlot—who has not even delivered herself, like Dekker's Bellafront, of much eloquent repentance in blank-verse and couplet. No wonder that this Cleopatra is judged to have two physiognomies that are irreconcilable! Only they are not physiognomies that ever look at us out of the play; they are importations there from the little stock of masks approved by the tribe to which Professor Schücking belongs.

And the tribe has no ears. At some long-past seminar these organs have disappeared during an initiatory rite. But—alas— to be seminared thus is to be, as far as a masculine grasp of Shakespeare is concerned, more unseminared than Mardian. For the poetry is the key—to Cleopatra's character as to all else.

> No going then,
> Eternity was in our Lippes, and Eyes,
> Bliss in our browes bent: none our parts so poore,
> But was a race of Heaven . . .

> Hee's speaking now,
> Or murmuring, where's my Serpent of old Nyle,
> (For so he cals me:) Now I feede my selfe
> With most delicious poyson. Thinke on me
> That am with Phoebus amorous pinches blacke,
> And wrinkled deepe in time . . .

> Ah (Deere) if I be so,
> From my cold heart let Heaven ingender haile . . .

Would ever poetic dramatist, building up for an audience sensitive to the overtones of verse a harlot before whom stretched but one and a predictable road, go to work so? Is this the language of Nanna and Pippa, of Doris and Dusty?[52] It is true that Cleopatra does not display her statecraft and knowledge of languages; that she is nowhere shown seriously discussing the children's education with Antony. She is a woman absorbed in

F

the mystery of sensuality. But that for her sensuality *is* a mystery, and not a trade, is shown by the poetry in which she spontaneously clothes it.

And just as it is not a harlot who speaks at the beginning of the play so it is no Thusnelda who speaks at the end.

> Go fetch
> My best attyres; I am againe for *Cydnus* . . .

> If she first meete the Curled *Anthony*
> Hee'l make demand of her, and spend that kisse
> Which is my heaven to have . . .

> The stroke of Death is as a Lovers pinch,
> Which hurts, and is desir'd.

In her great moments, in fact, Cleopatra says things very characteristic of her earlier self. And yet, of course, she is changed:

> Lord of Lords,
> Oh infinite Vertue, comm'st thou smiling from
> The worlds great snare uncaught?

> Oh Sunne,
> Burne the great Sphere thou mov'st in, darkling stand
> The varrying shore o' th' world . . .

> The Crowne o' th' earth doth melt. My Lord!
> Oh wither'd is the Garland of the Warre,
> The Souldiers pole is falne: young Boyes and Gyrles
> Are levell now with men: The oddes is gone,
> And there is nothing left remarkable
> Beneath the visiting Moone.

> For his Bounty,
> There was no winter in't. An *Anthony* it was,
> That grew the more by reaping: His delights
> Were Dolphin-like, they shew'd his backe above
> The Element they liv'd in: In his Livery
> Walk'd Crownes and Crownets: Realms and Islands were
> As plates dropt from his pocket . . .

> Give me my Robe, put on my Crowne, I have
> Immortall longings in me. Now no more
> The juyce of Egypts Grape shall moyst this lip.
> Yare, yare, good *Iras*; quick: Me thinkes I heare
> *Anthony* call: I see him rowse himselfe

> To praise my Noble Act. I heare him mock
> The lucke of *Caesar*, which the Gods give men
> To excuse their after wrath. Husband, I come:
> Now to that name, my Courage prove my Title.
> I am Fire, and Ayre . . .

"I see him rowse himselfe to praise my Noble Act. I heare him mock the lucke of *Caesar*." If once more we are made aware that Cleopatra—in the somewhat bald phrase of Professor Stoll—is "still the same old girl" we are aware also of holding her in a new estimation, and one disconcerting to our traditional social judgments. In what she says there is a trick of the old rage—*veteris vestigia flammae*—but our preponderant impression is of a woman who has achieved an unexpected spiritual stature. Now, if earlier we had been shown Cleopatra (like a figure in another Roman tragedy) "sitting in a thoughtful posture: in her hand Plato's book on the Immortality of the Soul," the play would be less disconcerting to Professor Schücking, but at the same time it would fail of a principal effect. Cleopatra has appeared a wanton, sunk beyond recall in a barren dream of sense; and only her poetry has spoken of something else. And yet this something else was the truth of her; through her sterile sensuality there has subterraneously run the quickening stream; and here at last in her monument—to our feeling vast and oppressive as the Ptolemies' pyramids—like water cleaving the rock, her womanhood discloses itself in a mature and final splendour:

> Husband, I come . . .

> Peace, peace:
> Dost thou not see my Baby at my breast,
> That suckes the Nurse asleepe . . .

These are the simplicities of feeling upon which our awe and exultation at the end of the play are based.

8

"But"—the reply may come—"precisely so! And are not such stories of bad hats who in the end turn up trumps the staple of every cinema? Doubtless they represent, as you say, an escape from the tyranny of institutionalised behaviour-patterns, from society's insistence that we should suit the general convenience by unremittingly running true to form. But such stories are fantasies which depend not at all upon any psychological facts. For the artifice projected upon the screen evokes or releases the same emotions whether or not there be a correspondence with men as they are; and it is the emotion which counts, not the mechanism by which it is conjured into being. Granted that Shakespeare knew his business much better than Professor Schücking supposes, it by no means follows that Cleopatra is a consistent creation. In the theatre it is enough that she is surprising, and that she satisfies some obscure demand for vicarious regeneration. And how naïve the appeal to the poetry as validating the fable! Admittedly it is the poetry that constitutes the end of *Antony and Cleopatra* what it is. It is on the poetry that a convincing Cleopatra is finally borne from us as on some liberating and enlarging element. When we yield ourselves to the spectacle on the stage, or to the memory of it, and ourselves feel liberated and enlarged, it is the power of the poetry, finely spoken, that holds us in its spell. But the poetry, in a last analysis, is no more than an immemorial equivalent of that vast and hypnotically glittering silver screen which the Warner Brothers spread out before us in their palaces. Or the poetry is a dazzle-paint such as they put upon warships, a scintillating integument which distracts from or obscures the form and movement of what lies behind it. A child who believes that the magician has really sawn the lady in half, and who appeals for confirmation to the glitter of the tool employed, is scarcely less rational than yourself when you call the poetry into court to witness to the humanity of Shakespeare's characters."

In some such words as these, I fancy, a sympathetic critic might come to Schücking's assistance.

9

What are we to rejoin here? We may remark that when we have seen such a film as is described, and when upon a few minutes' reflection our experience prompts us to reject it as being no true representative fiction, we come from the cinema irritated and angry—and the more so if shortly before we have been weeping into a handkerchief. It would appear, then, that for right artistic satisfaction in a fable of this kind we *must* feel that there is a true imitation of actions such as do occasionally in life declare the ability of individuals under certain circumstances to transcend their definition or rôle. For though something like the emotions raised by this true imitation can be raised by an arbitrary contrivance the final impression is different. We are not content with an escape at any price from the world of straitened behaviour-patterns which society asserts. We require what our intuition declares to be verisimilar. And the film, although it may evoke a greater measure of crude emotion, we judge artistically inferior to, say, Conrad's *Lord Jim*. The end of *Antony and Cleopatra* is very moving—but assuredly no man on leaving the theatre ever thrust his wet handkerchief angrily away and ground his teeth at being cozened by a counterfeit of human passion. On the contrary, we are convinced of a profound significance in what we have witnessed. And we may assert— contemplating still the close of the play—that our impression of truth in the fable results not from an illusion which the poetry creates but from an actual correlation between high dramatic poetry and insight into substantial human nature. For true poetry is emotion differentiating, is passion clarifying itself, is the contemplation of these activities. And passion and convention are antithetical; it is in passion that the dancer breaks from the pattern, the player transforms his part, the pristine personality frees and declares itself. Poetry and a fresh revelation of human capacities therefore go naturally together, and in drama the poetry constantly speaks of the power of the individual, for long subdued or habituated to his own familiar image, to break through to orders of experience not familiar or worldly, and in which the ordinary bounds and limits of "character" as prescribed by custom and time may be profoundly modified. And yet, though modified, they persist, and control the manner in which the individual may transcend himself. Does not the essence of the last scene of *Antony and Cleopatra* consist partly at least in this observation of the continuing grip of "character": that for Cleopatra Antony's death after the high Roman fashion would be indeed impossible, a piece of theatrical psychology such as we reject in a film, but that she yet contrives her own heroism, exploiting an exotic and womanly ritual of robe and crown to dredge up attitudes and potencies that ordinarily lie sunk and obscured below her grasp?

In Cleopatra hidden depths move and declare themselves; that these could not be there is an arbitrary culture-assertion; that they are there the poetry witnesses. And Professor Schücking's estimate appears to me to be fatal to much of the persuasiveness of his thesis. His book is certainly to be esteemed on account of the many pioneer observations on pre-Shakespearian dramatic convention that it makes. But we must surely hold suspect an approach to drama which brings the student where—in Lascelles Abercrombie's phrase—"no conceivable audience of human beings" could arrive.[53] And the deficiency in approach can be traced. In place of adequate submission to the verse, and adequate examination of the concept of character in poetic drama, there has been substituted a system of preconceptions based on something we can know little about: the influence which current theatrical standards and expectations were likely to exert upon one whose art was to become a possession for all time.

CHAPTER V

"STEEP TRAGIC CONTRAST"

It was the owl that shriek'd, the fatal bellman
Which gives the stern'st good-night.

MACBETH, II, ii, 4

What I tell you three times is true.

THE BELLMAN

THE leading exponent of the new realism in Shakespeare
studies is Professor Elmer Edgar Stoll. No one has ever
been more pertinacious in enforcing a critical theory of the plays.
His erudition is noble and a little daunting; as I turn over his
numerous monographs and volumes of collected essays I am
alarmed by the length to which he has contrived to expand his
thesis, by this and even by the mere foot-pounds of physical
energy which the providing of the cross-references must have
entailed. Matthew Arnold was persuaded that one cannot always
be studying one's own works, but I do not know that Mr. Stoll
feels this: in his recent *From Shakespeare to Joyce* he gives more
than a hundred invitations to consult previous writings of his
own. And I am reminded as I read of something else which
Arnold said in the same place:

. . . it is not in my nature,—some of my critics would rather say,
not in my power,—to dispute on behalf of any opinion, even my
own, very obstinately. To try and approach truth on one side
after another, not to strive or cry, nor to persist in pressing forward,
on any one side, with violence and self-will,—it is only thus, it
seems to me, that mortals may hope to gain any vision of the
mysterious Goddess, whom we shall never see except in outline,
but only thus even in outline. He who will do nothing but fight
impetuously towards her or his own, one, favourite, particular line,
is inevitably destined to run his head into the folds of the black
robe in which she is wrapped.[54]

For many years Mr. Stoll has had his particular line, and he is a very good fighter, although handicapped by a style obscuring what proves, in fact, a reassuringly simple and compassable stock of ideas. I consider here a paper in which these ideas are fairly fully expressed. It is called "Source and Motive in *Macbeth* and *Othello*."[55] If what is there propounded proves unacceptable, then Mr. Stoll, while remaining a learned and acute commentator on drama in general, cannot, I judge, be accepted with much confidence as a new guide to Shakespeare. But at least he is a more interesting writer than numerous Bradley-and-water critics who have largely ignored him. Had Mr. Stoll been attended to as he deserved he might have said less alarmingly often what it has been his to say.

I

Stoll begins by observing that Shakespeare is himself artistically responsible for what is represented in *Othello* and *Macbeth*, since he is constrained neither by his audience's sense of historical fact nor by expectations based on previous dramatisings of the stories. If he departs from Cinthio and Holinshed the impulsion must lie in his own sense of what is dramatic. And he does depart from them widely and similarly in point of motivation. What then is the dramatic principle at work?

In *Macbeth*, the argument continues, Shakespeare would seem to put the hero much further beyond the reach of our sympathy than Holinshed does. For Holinshed explains that the Scottish monarchy was not strictly hereditary and that Macbeth had some reasonable hope of the crown until thwarted by Duncan's declaring for Malcolm; that Duncan's administration had been "feeble and slouthfull"; and that Macbeth, after slaying him without treachery or violating the laws of hospitality, "set his whole intention to maintaine justice and to punish all enormities and abuses which had chanced" and ruled justly and efficiently for ten years. All this, which might serve to extenuate his hero's criminality, Shakespeare discards. And he makes Duncan a trusting and gracious figure; the scene of his foul assassination Macbeth's own castle; the issue for Scotland an immediate and ever-rising bath of blood; the fatal deed itself neither preluded by any substantial aspiring to the royal power and envisaging of its attractions, nor succeeded by any satisfaction however fleeting in its attainment. "As Mr. Firkins and even Mr. Bradley have observed," Macbeth seems to be more aware of deterrents than incentives. Massively built up in terms of bravery or virtue at the beginning (and these qualities, with a large poetry, create sympathy and constitute a sort of goodness on the stage), he goes in horror to his crime and with horror remembers it. "The conscience in him, before and after, is that of a good man." And so, after Shakespeare has manipulated his source, the situation yields "a contrast big and sharp enough." But it is what we may call a stagy contrast. For any verisimilitude in Macbeth's fall from virtue to criminality fails as soon as we "pause to take notice how unpsychological the change . . . is."

Shakespeare, then, at once enlarges the wickedness of Macbeth's deed and diminishes its sober credibility. And if we are inclined to any reaching out after fact and reason in point of motivation he seems content to bring us up against the imponderable factor of the supernatural prompting by the prescient women. We cannot, since they are out of nature, set a limit to the power of their solicitations; and the odds against Macbeth, being thus incalculable, permit of the impression that his nobility is, after all, in some sort unimpaired.

2

In *Macbeth* there are witches; in *Othello*, Stoll says, there is a devil in the flesh. And Iago's function too is that of confronting the hero with a soliciting to evil so supernaturally potent as virtually to absolve. This devil's malignity is invisible and invulnerable, so that Othello could not do other than succumb. And the point is emphasised by relieving the devil of any substantial human occasion for his ill-doing; he acts not from motives but from a constituting principle and thus stands outside the bounds of a realistic psychology.

Now, just this Iago, Stoll goes on, is Shakespeare's invention, not Cinthio's. For Cinthio's Ensign has provocation enough for his villainy, which he aims not directly at the Moor but at Desdemona who has rejected his advances and at the Captain (Cassio) whom he believes that she loves. In this there is a substantial internal motive for his wickedness. But Shakespeare's Ancient has only the grudge of a man who has missed promotion; with him any powerful prompting from sexual jealousy is reduced to the dimensions of excuse and afterthought.

And it is not only Cinthio's Ensign who is modified, it is also his Moor:

> Moreover, though Cinthio's Moor is given some noble and attractive traits, especially at the outset, Shakespeare's is both there and throughout on a far higher level of intelligence and feeling. He is not a stupid dupe or a vulgarly vindictive cuckold. He is not the man to call the informer in to do the killing, or the concealing of it afterwards. For his own safety Shakespeare's, unlike Cinthio's Moor, shows no concern. Nor is there, for that matter, the slightest evidence in his conduct or his utterance, nor in the woman's either, of the love Iago suspects between him and Emilia. . . . On the contrary, the black man is made the grandest and noblest of Shakespeare's lovers; and it is only through Iago's overwhelming reputation for honesty and sagacity, the impenetrableness of his mask together with the potency of his seductive arts, that he is led astray and succumbs.

Thus in both *Macbeth* and *Othello*, we are told, the sources are wrested to give the same essential spectacle, that of "the brave and honourable man suddenly and squarely—and fatally—turned against the moral order," and this contrary to all psychological prediction, so that we are required to accept as a power setting the drama in motion evil forces which are independent of and more irresistible than any common and explicable human malevolence. Thus of realistic motive we must say that "the omission is deliberate and intentional, and the contravention of psychological probability is so as well." For when we dispassionately look at the tragedy, or fall, of Macbeth and Othello we are constrained to admit that

> neither change is probable. In neither is there much of what can be called psychology. In life neither person would really have done what he did. . . . The hero's conduct, at the heart of the action, is . . . not in keeping with his essential nature but in contrast with it.

And Shakespeare is responsible for deliberately contriving this. The stories as told in his sources have much more of sober likelihood.

3

But why, Stoll asks, in *Macbeth* and *Othello* does Shakespeare exhibit this spectacle of one inexplicably violating "his essential nature"? Because the excellence of the drama depends on the width of the gap between conduct and essential nature that the artifice of the playwright can persuade us—while still in the theatre—to accept. The thrill (and what the playwright is after is a thrill) comes from "the *good* man doing the deed of horror" —and the biggest thrill (we may legitimately infer from Stoll's thesis) will come from the best man doing the worst deed that we will at all swallow for the time. Thus Shakespeare chiefly seeks a kind of "emotional effect, with which psychology or even simple narrative coherence often considerably interferes." For anything making the deed less unlikely will necessarily make it, in this sense, less effective too.

> Manifestly—and, if not forthwith, certainly upon a moment's consideration—by all the motives prompting or circumstances attending the murder of Duncan that have been omitted, the big, sharply outlined, highly emotional contrast in the situation of a good man doing the deed of horror would be broken or obscured. If Macbeth had been thwarted or (to use Holinshed's word) "defrauded," as having, at this juncture, a better title to the throne than Malcolm, or had thought himself better fitted to rule; or, again, if Duncan had not borne his faculties so meek and been so clear in his great office, as in the tragedy but not the chronicle he is; why, then, Macbeth's conduct in killing him would have been more reasonable and more psychologically in keeping, to be sure, but less terrible, less truly tragic.

The dramatist seeks primarily what is surprising and so productive of vivid sensation. It is to provide vivid sensation that the playhouses open their doors—"life must be, as it has ever been, piled on life, or we have visited the theatre in vain." That Othello should do what he does is (though Stoll does not use the word in this sense) "sensational" and in this there is satisfaction provided the illusion for the moment holds. That our emotion is one with which "psychology" would "interfere" need in no way disturb us. For "the object of poetry is to enthral," Longinus says, and the business of the drama is to o'erstep the modesty of nature, or at least to give us "what from life we do not get—enlargement, excitement, another world, not a copy of this."

But lest we should think plainness the special ornament of this contention (which might stand as an unaffected plea for *Tarzan of the Apes*) Stoll immediately conjures about it that darkness with which he still labours to be shadowed:

> In both *Macbeth* and *Othello*, then, it is the whole situation that is mainly important, not the character; it is the reciprocal matter of motivation (whether present or missing), of defects or qualities in both victim and victimizer together. . . . And that airy edifice, an imaginative structure, is the emotionally consistent action or situation as a whole—the conduct of characters both active and passive, perhaps also a motivation both external and internal, but in any case a combination of interrelations or circumstances as important as the motives themselves; not to mention the apportionment of emphasis or relief whether in the framework or the expression, the poetry which informs both, and the individuality of the speech, which, real, though poetical, leads one to accept and delight in the improbable things said or done.

What are we to say of the simplified Shakespeare who thus naïvely peers at us from amid the jungle of Mr. Stoll's complicated prose?

4

It is perhaps fair to pause here and remark that Mr. Stoll is by no means to be charged with the absolute innovation of the ideas to which he gives currency in this paper and elsewhere. Gustav Rümelin, writing three-quarters of a century earlier, presents a markedly similar theory of Macbeth:

> The dramatic treatment in *Macbeth* offers but small scope for realistic criticism, since . . . supernatural powers are employed, against which there can be no pragmatic criticism. . . . More serious difficulties occur in the character of Lady Macbeth. Her demeanour before the deed and after it appears to violate that psychological law of essential unity and consistency of character to which Shakespeare in general, although with some exceptions, adheres. The workings of conscience in her case are magical and demoniacal, and not psychologically conceivable. . . . In the char-

acter of Macbeth, wonderfully and strikingly as he is depicted, we miss something also. Before he falls into temptation he is represented by the poet as of a noble nature, as we gather not only from his own deportment, but more clearly from the esteem in which he is held by the king and others. We have a right to expect that this better nature would reappear; after his glowing ambition had attained its end he ought to have made at least one attempt, or manifested the desire, to wear his ill-gotten crown with glory, to expiate or extenuate his crime by sovereign virtues. We could then be made to see that it by no means follows that evil must breed evil, and that Macbeth must wade on in blood in order not to fall. But . . . the nobler impulses of former days never for one moment influence him. Here too, as frequently elsewhere, Shakespeare exaggerates the contrast, and the effect, at the expense of psychological truth [*Auch hier überspannt Shakespeare den Contrast und den Effekt auf Kosten der psychologischen Wahrheit*]. . . . And yet all such criticisms cannot keep us from pronouncing Shakespeare's *Macbeth* the mightiest and most powerful of all tragedies.[56]

It is at once clear that Rümelin is very close to Stoll's

> This, of course, is not what we call motivation, not psychology.
> . . . But the contrast is kept clear and distinct; and the emotional
> effect—that the whole world has acknowledged.

Nevertheless there is a radical difference between these two verdicts. In Rümelin's view the psychological incoherence frequently found in Shakespeare is a defect and chargeable (as by Schücking) upon the primitive and popular character of his art. But for Stoll the psychological incoherence turns out to be an aesthetic and dramatic virtue of the most classical and orthodox sort.

5

We may pause to note too another earlier examination of *Macbeth* which advances considerations similar to Stoll's—though like Rümelin's rather by way of stricture than of apology and revelation. It is to be found in that essay of Robert Bridges's the main tenets of which I have tried to discuss earlier. And Bridges, it seems to me, presses somewhat further than either Stoll or Rümelin into the heart of the play, and, by giving a deeper view of matters for which we must account, better prepares the ground for an adequate conclusion.

In *Measure for Measure*—Bridges will be recalled as arguing
—a coherent psychology is sacrificed to the exigencies of a
striking story, pleasing to an unsophisticated audience. So too
with *Macbeth*. But whereas in *Measure for Measure* the psychological incoherence is patent, in *Macbeth* Shakespeare devises
means to conceal it.

How comes it that such a man as Macbeth commits such
crimes? Shakespeare has no real answer, no "plain psychological
conception," and his method of dealing with the point is not so
much to reveal as to confuse. "Judging from the text, he does
not wish us to be clearly determined as to whether Macbeth's
ambition had preconceived and decided on the murder of Duncan; or whether the idea was chiefly imposed upon him by a
supernatural devilry; or whether he was mainly urged to it by
his wife, and was infected and led by her." Thus the effects
obtained, although magnificent, are procured by a deception.
And of the tragedies in general it may be said that Shakespeare
is perpetually obliged to surprise his audience; to attain this he
will risk, or even sacrifice, the logical and consistent; but in the
theatre the inconsistency must not appear, and so Shakespeare
develops a technique for obscuring it. For example, for some
cardinal action in a play various possible motives will be hinted at
and prominence given now to one possibility and now to another
as is convenient. Thus through shifts of conduct inconsistent
with any one motive we always have some congruous motive in
focus, and we are seduced from the attempt at any final elucidation
by Shakespeare's convincing verisimilitude and richness of detail.

> Having found a story the actions of which were suitable, Shake-
> speare adopted them very much as they were, but remade the
> character of the actor. In the original story the actor would be
> known and judged by his actions: this Shakespeare reverses by first
> introducing his hero as a man superior to his actions; his art being
> to create a kind of contrast between the two, which has, of course,
> no existence in the original tale; and his success depends on the
> power and skill with which this character is chosen and enforced
> upon the audience; for it is when their minds are preoccupied with
> his personality that the actions follow as unquestionable realities,
> and, in the *Macbeth*, even preordained and prophesied.

This use of contrast, Bridges continues, holds nothing illegiti-
mate or even peculiar in itself; and art here only calls for modera-

tion. But Shakespeare, in the hunt for surprise that shall border on sensation, pushes the technique beyond discretion. *Some* element of the unexpected in a man's actions, *some* disparity between these and his character, is natural in drama. But "it cannot be conceded that any character is capable of any action: there is a limit, and Shakespeare seems to delight in raiding across it." The murder of Duncan is such a raid. In the history Macbeth kills Duncan in a soldierlike manner; in the play the circumstances are such as to entail the most dastardly violation of honour. For the sake of theatrical excitement the gap between character and action has been widened beyond credibility.

With this we may say that Stoll agrees. But for Stoll Shakespeare in all this is pursuing the legitimate aims of drama, and his artifices to this end are a virtuosity to be rejoiced in. Bridges regards them as a "dishonesty."

6

The problem is now tolerably distinct. In Shakespeare—and typically in *Macbeth* and *Othello*—there is something like a deliberate omitting of clear and sufficient motives for action, there is a lack of discernible correspondence between the man and his deed. And in place of such an unimpeachable "psychology" we are offered the "steep tragic contrast" afforded by men arbitrarily precipitated into situations to which they could by no means bring themselves; we are offered this and behind it—lest we should begin inconveniently to use our wits before we are out in the street again—now external forces of irresistible evil and now a sort of finessing technique in which motives are advanced and then withdrawn before their weight can be estimated. And this we are offered in the interest of *sensation*, which Bridges condemns and Stoll approves—declaring that "it is not primarily to present characters in their convincing reality that Shakespeare and the Greeks have written . . . but to set them in a state of high commotion."

Now, if this be how the matter stands with Shakespeare there can be little doubt (it appears to me) that Bridges's is the juster verdict on his art. For it is surely no good setting characters in commotion, however high, that is simply commotion *per se*; the

commotion must be a specific commotion, and the character—
at some level of his being—apt to it, or the effect will not be truly
tragic. There is high commotion in Webster, but we could
reassort the masks and the emotions without much loss. There
is high commotion in the heroic plays of Dryden, but we may
doubt whether any man came from that theatre feeling rapt to the
heights of art.

It is true, of course, that the theory of drama as an impossible,
and for that very reason piquant, medley or concatenation
of emotions has its own aesthetic behind it, one expressed
compendiously enough by Francis Bacon when he declared that

> Imagination . . . may at pleasure join that which nature hath severed,
> and sever that which nature hath joined; and so make unlawful
> matches and divorces of things.[57]

And it is true that there is support for this reading in the fact that
dramatic poetry demonstrably presents the mechanisms of the
mind and passions not always as we familiarly hold them to be.
But this reading, when pursued, degrades dramatic poetry against
our deeper sense of it, leaving us (as Bridges discerns) nothing
but *poetry*—and poetry basely or fatuously used. We are left,
indeed, with no more than an arbitrary fiction such as might be
arrived at with one of those devices sold to aspiring authors, in
which a dial inscribed with numerous characters and their attributes is spun upon a card giving a variety of plots, and as the
arrow falls so must the story be framed. With such a machine a
trained writer might contrive piquant fictions enough, but not
genius could make them last. For artifices such as Stoll describes
have surely not the life or enduringness of representative fictions,
and to view Shakespeare's plays as transcendentally clever con-
structions of this kind is really to give the sternest good-night of
all to the reputation of the dramatist. And against Bacon here,
and Mr. Stoll after him, we may wonder whether we may not set
the words of a more catholic critic:

> The irregular combinations of fanciful invention may delight
> for a while, by that novelty of which the common satiety of life
> sends us all in quest; but the pleasures of sudden wonder are soon
> exhausted, and the mind can only repose on the stability of truth.

I must now try to show that "the stability of truth" does,
after all, underlie the motivation in *Macbeth*.

7

Macbeth is set (as Rümelin has it) in a "region of hoary eld" [*auf den . . . Boden einer grauen Vorzeit*]; it is a drama filled with darkness, the supernatural, sleep and dreams. And by means of these, Bradley says,

> Shakespeare has concentrated attention on the obscurer regions of man's being, on phenomena which make it seem that he is in the power of secret forces lurking below, and independent of his consciousness and will.

The treatment of motive in the play will be found, I think, to follow from this. Macbeth's rational motives are made insufficient, elusive, contradictory, in order to bring home to us not the mere thrill of evil but its tortuousness and terrifying reach; its beckoning presence just over the threshold of certain more than common natures.

"In *Macbeth*," writes Sir Edmund Chambers, "the central idea or theme seems to be this: A noble character, noble alike in potentiality and fruition, may yet be completely overmastered by mysterious, inexplicable temptation."[58] Now, whether this is indeed, as Stoll would maintain, "not what we call motivation, not psychology," or is tantamount, in Bridges's words, to making "any character capable of any action," depends on whether the inexplicability is felt as absolute or contingent. For the mysterious and the inexplicable—matter to the springs of which we can only very uncertainly grope our way—are part of our experience of nature; and the dramatist is not confined to what he can make thoroughly lucid. Macbeth, certainly, must not be inexplicable as real people are never inexplicable. But he may, and that very effectively, be inexplicable after the fashion in which his sort of person is often inexplicable. If we can say as we watch, "Were I such a man, and my circumstances these, then—terrible as is the thought and mysterious though it be to our small knowledge of the human soul—it might well be thus that I should act": if we can say this, the inexplicability is of that contingent kind found in nature and allowable in tragedy.

And when Bridges admits as allowable in tragedy "*some* element of the unexpected in a man's actions, *some* disparity

G

between these and his character," he shows himself aware of all this; much more aware than Stoll. But he contends that since Macbeth's crime is great, and by Shakespeare exacerbated, the gap between Macbeth and his deed is inordinate. Macbeth is not *remotely* the kind of man to kill Duncan as he does, and thus the element of the inexplicable here is no perception and acknowledgment of the inexplicable in nature, but a mere violation of nature.

But we must wonder whether behind this conception of the moral character of Macbeth, as behind Stoll's, there be not an undue influence from the classical theory of drama. For it appears to me that both critics view Macbeth through the spectacles of the *Poetics* and thereby burden themselves with a steeper "tragic contrast" than did Shakespeare, who did not use the spectacles of any books. Aristotle judged it necessary that a tragic hero should be better than ordinary men, and that any fatal flaw which his character held should be such as yet to leave him superior to depravity or vice. Implicit in this view is the opinion that moral character is simple and measurable; just as to-day we may say that the most suitable man for a given task will be one with an intelligence quotient within such and such a range so does the classical theory of drama say that the most suitable man for the task of hero in a tragedy will be one with a morality quotient analogously definable. Bridges, when he feels that the nobility of Macbeth must be such as to preclude his committing—under any circumstances—an atrocious crime, is conceivably swayed by this all-of-a-piece conception of character. But in life, as we know, perhaps every personality is in some degree dissociated; and this fact of universal significance, which is given gross expression in certain pathological states, often finds a species of covert (and perhaps obscurely cathartic or therapeutic) release in art. There are, in a sense, two Macbeths; and the dichotomy is rendered to us both directly and in terms of the poetic structure. Macbeth commits crime upon crime: first, as he supposes, a crime of ambition and then, as we know, crimes of fear and spite; his reputation crumbles and the man who had won "golden opinions" is known for avariciousness and as a lecher. In this he is as the imagery of the play represents him: too small for his robes; he shrivels at their touch; they are envenomed, as we might suppose. Macbeth clips to himself the virtues of the Sagas and exhibits more than the power of the men who composed them; and here he is titanic, as the imagery also represents him, and abounds in qualities which we envy as we watch. Perhaps this particular contrast—the contrast between the criminal who murders Duncan and the man whose "magnificent qualities of mind, extreme courage, and poetic imagination" call for our admiration—ought not to exist in nature. But assuredly it does—being thereby not the less mysterious and awful (for the divine Abundance is often that), but only the more proper for dramatic representation.

And so Shakespeare did not, I suspect, conceive of Macbeth as good or bad *simpliciter*; the "obscurer regions" of the man held some antilogy too radical to make that a profitable approach. But Shakespeare did conceive of Macbeth as *imaginative* in all but the highest degree. And here indeed—in what Bradley calls his "excitable and intense, but narrow" imagination, with its extreme sensibility to sinister and morbid impressions—appears to me to be one of the cardinal facts of the play. Others are (1) his poetic genius and histrionic talent, inclining him to view his own conduct as a dramatic spectacle, (2) that archaic quality of the play whereby Shakespeare thrusts the action with an uncharacteristic obtrusiveness into a rude past, (3) the pervasiveness of images of bloodshed, so that the whole is seen, again in Bradley's words, "as through an ensanguined mist," (4) the speed with which the play hurries to an unusually early crisis. In all these we have, as it appears to me, the conditions for making the "inexplicable" element in the tragedy of that kind which beckons us towards an actual mystery in things, rather than of the kind which merely occasions a "sudden wonder" arresting for a day.

8

Perhaps much of all this is covered by the simple statement that in everybody there is some lurking force of evil ready to strike in a weak or unguarded hour. Sometimes this force hints its strength as we sleep:

> Mercifull Powers,
> Restraine in me the cursed thoughts that Nature
> Gives way to in repose . . .

>   wicked Dreames abuse
> The Curtain'd sleepe.

Sometimes it invades the waking mind in sinister fantasy:

> where's that Palace, whereinto foule things
> Sometimes intrude not? Who ha's that breast so pure,
> But some uncleanly Apprehensions
> Keepe Leetes, and Law-dayes, and in Sessions sit
> With meditations lawfull?

It can be potent in men of unimpaired moral perception; so inexplicably potent as to suggest mysterious solicitation exercised by an external malignant power (the witches, Iago, Iachimo). And, since this evil rises up in the form of horrible imaginings, it may be most overwhelming, and so, at a time of emotional stress, sweep on to action, in the most imaginative men—particularly in the man who is imaginative without the release of being creative. Macbeth is such a man. He and his wife are immensely potent, but their tragedy is a tragedy of sterility. Macbeth is such a man, exposed to exceptional emotional stresses.

The play opens upon rumour of battle, upon the assertion, as by a malevolent power, that

> Faire is foule, and foule is faire,

and then upon descriptions of war, rebellion, treachery and bloodshed in a semi-barbarous and disordered society. Bloodshed has brought Macbeth fair report: "Brave Macbeth," says the Captain, recounting the fight with the merciless Macdonwald,

> unseam'd him from the Nave to th' Chaps,
> And fix'd his Head upon our Battlements—

and King Duncan exclaims

> O valiant Cousin! worthy Gentleman!

With the Norwegian army Macbeth and Banquo have fought as if

> they meant to bathe in reeking Wounds,
> Or memorize another *Golgotha*—

and this report too smacks of honour to the king. Presently Macbeth himself steps on the stage as if straight from this blood-bath, dazed by it, and unconsciously echoing the words of the witches:

> So foule and faire a day I have not seene.

"*Foul* with regard to the weather," the commentators say, "and *fair* with reference to his victory." But it is also the victory alone, the snatching honour by unseaming people from the nave to the chaps, that is both foul and fair—a monstrous confusion from which Macbeth, imaginative and highly organised as well as a soldier, now emerges, battle-shocked. That night he kills a man for a kingdom.

Macbeth's castle was not really a politic place in which to murder the king, a fact observed by Bridges:

> Shakespeare, choosing that Duncan shall be secretly murdered, makes Lady Macbeth represent the advent of Duncan to their castle as a favourable opportunity; and he knows that the audience, blinded by the material juxtaposition, will regard it as such. Now to propose this dastardly violation of honour to Macbeth would, most probably, have stimulated his nobility and scared him from the crime however fully he might have been predetermined on it.

Why, does Lady Macbeth insist that "time and place" have made themselves *now*, and *here* at Inverness? It is partly because she sees that Macbeth's almost hypnoidal state is favourable; he is like a man moving in a blood-drenched trance, subject to visual and auditory hallucinations, uncertain of the boundaries of actuality and dream. And no doubt it is only another of the many ironies in this play that Lady Macbeth, exploiting a disorder akin to somnambulism in her husband now, herself falls a victim to the actual malady later on—when Macbeth himself has come horribly awake and will sleep no more. But chiefly it is because Lady Macbeth has a better understanding of the recesses of her husband's character than Stoll or Bridges succeeds in arriving at, and knows that the deeper criminality involved in violating a "double trust" will indeed scare him, but will compel more than it scares.

The abyss of evil is very real to Macbeth, and the deeper it is, the more luridly lit from below, the more it fascinates him as a dramatic spectacle in which he is obscurely called to engulf himself. The thought of murdering Duncan, first or new glimpsed in the recesses of his mind at the prompting of the witches, produces violent somatic disturbance, as the prospect of a ritual act of cannibalism may do in a Kwakiutl Indian. Nor is the parallel so outlandish as it may appear. For it is veritably the crime and not the crown that compels Macbeth, as it is the virtue that lies in the terrible and forbidden, and not the flavour of human flesh, that compels the savage. And Macbeth's mind is darkened and groping. For what effects the commission of a crime—criminology declares—is less a motive than a confluence of motives, the more potent of which may be only confusedly, if at all, within the conscious awareness of the perpetrator. And when Macbeth momentarily fights his way from the "obscurer regions" of his soul, when he would vindicate his action in other terms than that of "secret forces lurking below, and independent of his consciousness and will," he knows that he has returned to a region in which there is no effective spur to his intent; and he knows when his crime is committed that it is absolutely futile. He has been betrayed by his intensely realising imagination, in itself a splendid thing, which, in a period of weakened rationality, has exhibited himself to himself as the central figure in a drama colossally evil. He has vividly seen not his true self but a treacherous criminal *persona* risen from its lurking-place below the threshold of the diurnal Macbeth; it stalks before him, a gigantic shadow, into Duncan's chamber; it plays its part in a nightmarish festival of blood; and then it deserts him. He goes to the deed on the wings of a vast self-dramatising rhetoric. "'Twas a rough night," he mutters, tight-lipped and appalled, when the deed is done.

The "gap," then, which Stoll distinguishes between the man and his deed does, in a sense, exist. But that it is matter of psychological fact and not merely of theatrical fancy the following citation from a textbook of criminology may serve to enforce:

> It is still not sufficiently realised that the criminal at the moment of the act is a different man from what he is after it—so much so that one would sometimes think them different beings. . . . Our psychological judgment, our instinct as well as our experience, seem to tell us sometimes that the deed does not belong to the doer nor the doer to the deed. Nevertheless the act must be an expression of the criminal's mental tension, must spring from his mental condition, must have promised gratification to his psychological needs. We are faced by a riddle as long as we do not know what motive actuated him. In many cases, and especially in the most serious crimes, he can, with the best will in the world, give us but inadequate information; he is unable to establish a connection between the deed and his personality.[59]

One could scarcely find a better commentary than this on the problem of Macbeth's crime. As has been said in an admirable place:

> Our unknown selves in life are sometimes more potent than our known. And that also should be a principle, among many others, of the art of Shakespeare interpretation.[60]

9

We cannot, I think, get away in tragedy from the strange fact of the interplay of conscious and unconscious motive and from the species of release which the exhibition of that interplay brings to an audience keyed to poetic apprehension. And yet a Macbeth mysteriously prompted from archaic strata of the mind will appear to many as something improper to dramatic poetry—as constituting, in fact, what Bridges, in another connection, calls "a pathological study which cannot hold our respect." And Stoll, who will have no psychology at all in *Macbeth*, expressly excludes this kind:

> The only psychology possible for Macbeth is a morbid or abnormal sort, which would have him tempted by the sight of cold steel to plunge it into you, or by an abyss to jump into it; but that, not clearly indicated, is out of the question for a popular tragic hero in the time of Elizabeth.

But at least we may suspect that any view of tragedy which chiefly canvasses what is "clearly indicated" will be in danger of being a superficial view, and will take us no further with Attic drama than with Elizabethan. And, indeed, I repeat that it is Aristotle's grand rationalising of Attic drama (epic, he says, will tolerate more of the "irrational" than drama) rather than the direct experience of Shakespeare that discernibly sways the critics, and sets them seeking for the plausible ἁμαρτία in the known and ponderable character to the neglect of those terrifying, surprising but authentic shadows of our unknown selves which the penetrating rays of the poetic drama cast upon the boards before us. And if it still be urged that this line of argument substitutes a clinical for a tragic Macbeth I can only reply that the fascination and horror of bloodshed, particularly the fascination and horror of bloodshed in certain localities, are counterpoised forces not in the merely diseased mind but in the primitive, which is now the underlying, mind; and as such they are always potentially eruptive in traumatic situations. Here is the fundamental mechanism or motive beneath the superficial incentives prompting Macbeth, and it is to bring the former sufficiently near the surface of the complex whole that Shakespeare disburdens the fable of much of the weight of the latter.

But Shakespeare not only neglects conscious motives; he blurs them—as Bridges, going deeper, discerns. And the explanation must lie, I think, in the fact that an intellectual as well as emotional confusion attends such a deed as the killing of Duncan. The "veiled confusion of motive" to which Bridges points, the indefiniteness as to when and in whose mind the idea of the crime first started up, echoes this. The blurring is indeed deliberately put into the play, and is achieved by devices that would be impossible in a naturalistic drama. Thus when Shakespeare secures the effect of there having been, and not been, a previous plot between Macbeth and his wife, he is certainly deserting nature for artifice. Why? In order to secure, I would suppose, by a non-realistic device such as he is always prepared to use, a dramatic correlative to the confusion in Macbeth's mind. If the audience can be made to grope among motives which are insubstantial, phantasmagoric and contradictory they will be approximating to the condition of the protagonist. There is no "dishonesty" here; there is only a subtle and powerful art. And it is an art constantly used in the interest of realising a *man* —an individual at once unique and representative, caught, as all men may be, in some giant's grasp from the infra-personal levels of his own being.

I conclude, then, that before *Macbeth* we ought not to abandon the conception of a "psychology" (as Mr. Stoll would have us do) but deepen it. The "steep tragic contrast" of which we are indeed made powerfully aware results not from arbitrary contrivance but from the acknowledgment, lucid to our active imagination, that

> O the mind, mind has mountains; cliffs of fall
> Frightful, sheer, no-man-fathomed.

And—as Hopkins adds—

> Hold them cheap
> May who ne'er hung there.

In the theatre we do not hold them cheap; it is only in the study, or before a blackboard, that it occurs to us to believe that we have been cozened by a fiction. And to insist that we are wiser men when delivering lectures, or when annotating some new dissertation out of one written in 1915, than we are when actually subject to the experience that Shakespeare created for us, is an assumption which, in a critic however comprehensively read, cannot but suggest a somewhat narrow or insulated sensibility.

Much of what I have said here holds, too, of *Othello*. Only in *Othello* Shakespeare's anatomy of the soul, his exposure of the "hidden man," is accomplished by a bolder technique of dissection than that employed in *Macbeth*, a technique which must considerably modify—although not at all in Stoll's direction—our notion of the relationship that his art posits between some of his *dramatis personae* and individual human beings.

10

The case against the plausibility of *Othello* begins with Thomas Rymer, whose aspersions in *A Short View of Tragedy*, published in 1692, have had sufficient vitality to be commended by Mr. T. S. Eliot (in a two-line footnote) in 1924.[61] Rymer says that Shakespeare's object in the play is to surprise us with what is horrible and prodigious. To attain this end he resorts to a fable which is improbable and absurd, and to characters who are unnatural and lacking in all decorum. Othello, a Venetian general, does nothing in keeping; he shows no soldier's mettle, but gapes after every paltry insinuation and labours to be jealous —and when this laboured jealousy finally maddens him he deputes Iago to kill the rival and himself kills the silly unresisting woman. As for Iago it is certain that such a monster never existed; he has no reason to hate Desdemona: and to abet her murder has nothing of the soldier, the man, or nature in it. In fact the whole foundation of the play is monstrous, and produces nothing but horror and aversion. Shakespeare profanes the name of tragedy at the instigation of the illiterate audience of carpenters and cobblers for whom he wrote.

And something like Rymer's case is repeated by Bridges, who adds that for this audience given over to gross sensation and surprise the complaisant dramatist even took some care to avoid reasonable motives as he went along:

> And how easy it would have been to have provided a more reasonable ground for Othello's jealousy. If in the break in the second act his vessel had been delayed a week by the storm, those days of anxiety and officious consolation would have given the needed opportunity, and the time-contradictions might also have been avoided.

If the tragedy is intolerably painful this is not merely because we see Othello being grossly deceived, but because we are ourselves constrained to submit to palpable deception. And particularly Iago is impossible, since a man with a tithe of his wickedness could not pass invisible as he does. Shakespeare aimed merely at sensation, but what was a pleasurable excitement for his obtuse audience is intolerable to us.

Both Rymer and Bridges take exception to *Othello* on what, finally, are moral grounds. But what initially repels both critics is the play's *unnaturalness*; they condemn in it very much what Johnson condemned in *Cymbeline*: "the folly of the fiction, the absurdity of the conduct . . . and the impossibility of the events in any system of life."[62]

Now, most criticism of *Othello*, if it does not ignore these impressions, endeavours to argue them away as incompatible with the evident greatness of the play, which requires that the characters should be humanly plausible and their motives sufficient. Thus for Bradley *Othello* is a profound play of individual character. The hero's very nobility—the fact that his trust, where he trusts, is absolute—makes him unusually open to deception; and, if once wrought to passion, he is likely to act with little reflection, with no delay, and in the most decisive manner conceivable. Iago, again, is a complex but credible figure. Certainly, to pass invisible as he does, his powers of dissimulation and of self-control must have been prodigious, but we may remark that he finds relief in those caustic or cynical speeches which, being misinterpreted, only heightened confidence in his honesty. He has a sort of spite against goodness, not from being a devil loving evil for evil's sake, but because to his egotistical philosophy goodness is a stupidity which nevertheless in a stupid world prospers and is popular. Lack of passion rather than some excess of it is the very horror of Iago. He is egotistical, cold, heartless, sensitive to slights, and his grand motive is a longing to satisfy the sense of power. We must acknowledge that perfectly sane people exist in whom fellow-feeling of any kind is so weak that an almost absolute egoism becomes possible to them, and with it the vices of ingratitude and cruelty. And we must acknowledge too that such evil appears to ally itself easily with exceptional powers of will and intellect. Iago's place is here; he is not absolute in evil but merely tries to see himself so; several flickering human compunctions are visible in him, and these serve to increase the essential verisimilitude of the picture.

All argument like this in favour of the human credibility of *Othello* Stoll turns down as a mere projecting upon Shakespeare's play of modern and historically erroneous ways of thinking.[63] Stoll is thus, in a sense, back with Rymer and Bridges, for whom the characters are unnatural and the motives insufficient or absurd. But, supporting and greatly broadening their indictment, Stoll nevertheless comes to a conclusion altogether different, and one which (he holds) would rehabilitate Shakespeare as a dramatist every whit as great as Bradley claims. Unfavourable criticism of Shakespeare—as also inept laudation—rests upon an insufficient consideration of the canons of dramatic art, and particularly of the admissible and indeed grateful difference between that art and real life. It is no condemnation of *Othello* to demonstrate that it has an impossible time-scheme, or that the hero's progress from being "free and open" to being insanely jealous is something holding no correspondence with known psychological forces, or that the impenetrability of Iago's villainy is a mere arbitrary convention no more related to things as they are than is the equally arbitrary convention of the impenetrability of Rosalind's or Kent's disguise. Nor need we be disturbed upon perceiving that Othello's trustfulness ("his trust, where he trusts, is absolute") requires *a fortiori* that he should trust his wife and friend at least as fully as a stranger. For in this of Othello's succumbing with incredible facility to Iago's deception we are in the presence, Stoll holds, not of psychology but of literary convention, of a dodge for getting a good story going. The convention of the calumniator believed is as old as the story of Potiphar's wife or of the wicked counsellors of Germanic heroic legend, and here in Shakespeare's tragedy it "summarily, theatrically lifts us over contradiction and paradox as over a rock in the river." For the tragedy of *Othello* is an "airy edifice" owing more to artifice than intuition, in which the operation and inter-action of the passions are triumphantly freed from the trammels of psychology, with the result that massive emotional effects are produced in a pleasing independence of the life of everyday, but always with an appearance of coherence and plausibility within the framework of the illusion.

Is it possible to feel that before Stoll's scrutiny the idealised Othello of Bradley must be abandoned, but that some other interpretation of the play may be found which shall make it significant as representative fiction?

II

There is one evident weakness in Stoll's argument, here as elsewhere. In considering such immemorial themes as that of the calumniator believed he nowhere presses beyond the conception of their being arbitrary devices for starting a yarn. His general feeling seems to be that the older the story the less correspondence will it hold with any realities of the human situation. But it is surely doubtful whether under this persuasion anything so ambitious as Comparative Literature can be successfully studied nowadays. And, at least, Comparative Literature not less than Comparative Religion requires as well as voluminous reading a clear head. Is it conceivable that Mr. Stoll has been too busy reading and rereading *Zaïre* and *Kabale und Liebe* (to say nothing of Horn, Ulrici, Bulthaupt, Vischer and Wetz) to have had leisure for the achieving of this necessary clarity? I suspect that if he came upon a Nativity at Mau and a Crucifixion at Pago-Pago he would discern in these evidence that Bethlehem and Calvary were merely arbitrary devices for starting a yarn. Whereas, of course, just as widespread nativity and crucifixion stories can, at least with an equal colour, be read as adumbrations and intima-tions of the central fact of history as Christianity views it, and therefore as being so many witnesses to the significance of that fact, just so can the pervasiveness in drama of the "calumniator believed" (as in *Much Ado* or *Cymbeline*, *Orlando Furioso*, *Philaster* or *The Conquest of Granada*) be read as witnessing to some central human predisposition by which these are prompted and sustained. Nor is this possibility invalidated by the patent absurdity or nullity of many calumniator-fictions, by their evident employment as indeed no more than a storyteller's resource. A convention, like a superstition, may represent a significant perception gone fossilised or inert. And to reanimate a convention, to strip it of sophistication so that its essence is again near the surface and working, is perhaps part of the instinct of the original artist.

And as with the fable so with the agent. Confronted with Iago, Stoll again takes it for granted that what is primitive (in the sense of being directly derived from a rudimentary art) is necessarily crude, superficial and—above all—"unpsychological" or without relevance to the depths. The primitive figure from whom Stoll rightly sees Iago as being, with a rather surprising directness, descended, he views as an arbitrary dummy constructed merely to curdle the blood.

But just so—we might reply to Stoll—may some monstrous idol or totem-pole appear, and yet such a thing is actually the product of a very vivid awareness of actual forces in the human psyche. And thus it may be with Iago. This invisible and indefeasible villain is indeed an immemorial standby in romance, but conceivably he earned his place there not as something stagy, delightfully and horrifically unreal; he earned his place there because he expresses a psychological truth. The error is in supposing that the mature and developed dramatist who dips into fairy-tale thereby dips into something other than human life. When we discard this notion we may see that the "calumniator-believed" theme, the importance of which Stoll accurately distinguishes, can, with all its seeming irrationality, have its place in a picture fully "psychological."

At this point we may conveniently consider the lines upon which modern psychology seems inclined to interpret the particular convention upon which the play is based.

12

Civilised man is obliged to live far beyond his moral income, and any appearance of stability and solvency which he presents is achieved only through much concealment and subterfuge. His difficulties indeed are such that in order to get along at all he has to ignore them, struggling to confine them within unconscious regions of his mind. Many of the great myths, including those concerning wars in and expulsions from heaven, express this situation. In fact it may be said that every man has his rebel angels, who will not willingly lie long upon the burning marl of a nether world; perpetually they strive by devious routes and guileful policy to gain and carry by assault the empyrean of the conscious mind, of the willed personality and its values. Mysteriously, the conscious man may know little of the battle; may know it only by the exhaustion it brings, or by finding that he bears about with him a secret and inexplicable wound. Part of the force of the assault, indeed, he may be able to exploit like a wrestler, and by this sublimation the dark angels will turn what engines he directs; to the world he will the more appear a tall man of his hands—artist or warrior or saint. But if the struggle becomes desperate the mind brings various emergency measures into play. Thus, and as if to clear itself of the guilt of forbidden impulses forcing a passage from below, it projects these impulses upon the person most injured by them; the mechanism being (as we have noted in an earlier instance): "It is not I but you who have this illicit thought or act to answer for." Hence the appearance in the conscious mind of irrational and baseless suspicions. But these suspicions are themselves surrounded by illicit impulses of jealousy, malevolence and destruction, and so the responsibility of instigating and feeding them may also upon the slightest excuse be projected upon some other person. And by thus endowing this other person with impulses working within itself the distraught mind immensely increases the potency for destruction of that person's every word and suggestion.[64]

These, it is held, are the actual facts of mind underlying the convention of the calumniator believed, and it is clear that, after a fashion not recognised by Stoll, they can be exploited to credibilise the fable of *Othello* at its most perplexing points: namely the flimsiness of the case against Desdemona and the resistlessness of Iago. Iago's villainy draws its potency from Othello's own mind; it is invisible to others because it is, in a sense, *not there*; the devil in the play, like all devils, represents a projection upon some comparatively neutral or insignificant thing; Iago is a device of Othello's by which Othello hears an inner voice that he would fain hear and fain deny. From this complex of ideas much argument can be drawn.

And all this matter is certainly, in my opinion, relevant; there is real light to be gained from it. But can we use it to interpret the play in terms which are, broadly regarded, naturalistic? I do not think that we can. Any attempt to view the play as presenting this picture of things in terms of simple realism—any attempt, that is to say, to rewrite Bradley with a hero drawn from the new psychology—encounters a very real difficulty to which I shall presently come. But first we may notice one or two such Othellos who have, in fact, of late been disengaged from the play.

13

An early Othello of this sort makes a brief and characteristically discreet appearance in an essay of Mr. T. S. Eliot's:

> What Othello seems to me to be doing in making this [his last] speech is *cheering himself up*. He is endeavouring to escape reality, he has ceased to think about Desdemona, and is thinking about himself. . . . Othello succeeds in turning himself into a pathetic figure, by adopting an *aesthetic* rather than a moral attitude, dramatizing himself against his environment. He takes in the spectator, but the human motive is primarily to take in himself. I do not believe that any writer has ever exposed this *bovarysme*, the human will to see things as they are not, more clearly than Shakespeare.[65]

Othello, in fact, is a habitual self-deceiver, and he believes Iago's calumny neither because there is a convention that he must do so in order to start a yarn (which is Stoll) nor because he is too noble to suspect evil (which is Bradley). He believes Iago's calumny because there is something in his nature which leads him to do so.

From this may be developed a variety of arguments endeavouring to rehabilitate a "psychological" Othello in terms of a more realistic (or disillusioned) view of human relationships than Bradley's. And acute observations can be made here. Iago everywhere passes as honest, but of four people to whom he declares or insinuates that Desdemona is unchaste only Othello himself is credulous! Must we not then admit a weakness in

Othello, a predisposition to suspicion and jealousy such as Stoll in common with many more orthodox critics is concerned to deny? Is not Othello, in fact, a sombre and searching study in the inner processes of romantic idealism, the portrait of a man who obstinately refuses to face reality? "When Shakespeare created Othello," says one critic who develops this argument,

> he was merely imitating a life that produces a Rousseau or a William Blake, romantic idealists who swing from overtrust to unjust suspicion in a twinkling. Emotional polarity is one of the commonest traits of humanity. We all have a touch of paranoia in us. To the extent that we acclaim our own greatness . . . to that extent do we suspect others. . . . Othello from the beginning is too much of a romantic idealist—in regard to himself and others. He considers human nature superior to what it actually is. He over-values Desdemona as much as he overvalues Iago—and himself.[66]

Here is one reading of a fact marked by Bradley: the enlargement almost to something colossal of the stature of the hero. This impression of Bradley's is simply a reflection of Othello's own god-pose, his refusal to see himself as ordinarily human. The mistake in criticism is to see him as he sees himself, when we ought to see a man wrapt in self-delusion, of a known psychological type in which overtrust speedily shifts to undertrust on the first provocation, loving not a real woman but an image of his own creating which is wholly at the mercy of his secret fears and suspicions, grotesquely holding to his own inflated vision of himself even amid ruin, declaiming of "bumbast Circumstance, horribly stufft with Epithites of warre," even with the knife at his own breast and his bride sprawled suffocated on her bed beside him.

Argument of this sort is pressed yet further by a writer less concerned, conceivably, with *Othello* in itself than with indicting Bradley as a misleader of undergraduates. Bradley, we are told, failed to approach the play even "with moderate intelligence" and fell indeed into a course of as "triumphant sentimental perversity as literary history can show."[67] But Bradley's "potent and mischievous influence" may be finally dissipated by showing that Othello, far from being a noble, free and open character fatally practised upon by a diabolically clever antagonist, is from the first a man eaten out by "a habit of approving self-dramatisation." Iago's superhuman arts are moonshine; Othello yields with such promptness as to make it plain that the mind that undoes him is not Iago's but his own; the main datum is not Iago's diabolic intellect but Othello's readiness to respond. And if Bradley is wrong so is Stoll. There is no arbitrary and "un-psychological" stroke effected for the sake of "steep tragic contrast," for the whole tone of the play is such that no develop-ment will be acceptable in Othello unless the behaviour it imposes on him is reconcilable with our notions of ordinary psycho-logical consistency. And on the basis of what premiss can that consistency be secured? We must be brought to see that beneath his self-idealising and sentimentalising ways, which are in fact "a disguise," Othello owns only an obtuse and brutal egotism. In his new situation as a married man, which brings problems far different from those of the "big wars," his self-pride quickly becomes stupidity—ferocious stupidity, an insane and self-deceiving passion. It is absurd in Bradley to give a whole lecture to Iago, who is no more than a bit of dramatic mechanism.

Something akin to these readings of *Othello* we have found feasible in *The Winter's Tale*, where Leontes's suppressed impulse to infidelity finds as it were excuse and licence by projecting the infidelity upon another. And a Leontes-Othello, or one deriving from T. S. Eliot's suggestion of a study in *bovarysme*, is less unlikely to have behaved as the play declares him to have behaved than is the noble Othello of Bradley.

14

And yet I do not think that this will quite do. The line of interpretation we have been following—one arguing for a com-plete and subtle naturalism—is unsatisfactory for this simple reason: that the play presents no psychological entity answering to Othello as he is here described. Othello's nobility—however related to other facets of the man which older critics may have inadequately acknowledged—is certainly not a "disguise," it is a reality set magnificently before us in both Venice and Cyprus. And of the parallel with Leontes we must remark (with Granville-Barker) that Shakespeare treats the King of Sicilia as a patho-logical case, in which normal human experience is grotesquely

H

distorted; whereas the feeling in *Othello* is quite different.[68] An *Othello* in which the hero virtually imposes upon Iago Iago's rôle might, I suppose, be written, but it is not given us by our experience of the play. This new Othello is not the Othello who appears before us on the stage; the man we see there (and are, I judge, by the dramatist meant to see) is much nearer to Bradley's Othello.

Moreover in this aspect of the simple impression made by the man, Bradley's Othello and Stoll's are one—the essential difference lying in Bradley's asserting that this Othello *could do it*, and Stoll's asserting that he *could not*. There seems to me to be great force in Stoll's assertion. If we insist, that is to say, on taking the play on the level of straightforward naturalism there is still something like the arbitrary wrenching of the character that Stoll posits, or the character is superior to the situation upon which he is precipitated. On the one hand Stoll's own interpretation, if we fall back upon it, leads us away from the feeling of the play, or from the weight of it, which intimates something other than a fanciful invention which may please for a while. On the other hand that developed psychological criticism which comes nearer to the roots of the play, and better renders its weight and inwardness, puts forward as Othello a man who does not, in fact, appear before us. How is this somewhat desperate contradiction to be resolved? Perhaps only, as I have hinted, by abandoning *naturalism*—although by no means abandoning *psychological truth*. In poetic drama substantial human truth may be conveyed by means other than those of an entire psychological realism. Shakespeare's plays are basically realistic. But they can artfully and powerfully incorporate elements which, though psychologically highly expressive, are not realistic in themselves. I conclude, therefore, that although the basis of the tragedy is indeed to be found in the inward significance of the "calumniator believed," yet Shakespeare's manner of revealing, or intimating, that significance is different from what I have so far supposed.

In all the argument which we have yet considered there is an element missing; and it is an element for the sharp consciousness of which—though not perhaps for a right understanding of which—we are much indebted to Stoll. I mean the element of artifice, of boldly unrealistic devices used to significant ends. In *Macbeth* we have seen such a device in the suggestion of there having been and not been a previous plot between Macbeth and his wife. But it is in *Othello*, the "most finite of the tragedies,"[69] super-ficially so devoid of symbolical content, that we are brought really hard up against the limits of Shakespeare's realism.

His instinct is to make of his plays the mirror of life and, broadly speaking, he sets about this by the methods of the naturalistic writer. But he is always ready to follow his intuition behind and beneath life's visible and tangible surfaces and at any time he will shake hands with probability and even possibility when beckoned from some further border of consciousness by an imaginative truth. We must remember the imagination. It is his instrument—and it works, Coleridge tells us, by dissolving and dissipating in order to re-create.[70] We may find an instance of the working of this power in the play's treatment of time.

The chronological contradictions which *Othello* displays when considered realistically go in point of strangeness beyond any-thing similar in Shakespeare. In Stoll's terms—or Bridges's—it comes to this: that Iago's plot can pass undetected only in the press of rapid action, but other elements in the story are plausible only if there is the contrary impression of a considerable efflux of time; and therefore Shakespeare juggles skilfully with his two clocks. But it strikes me that there is something inward about the oddity of the time-scheme in *Othello*. It is as if Iago only wins out because of something fundamentally treacherous in time, some flux and reflux in it which is inimical to life and love. Mr. Middleton Murry has a fine perception here when he sees that *Iago* and *time* are in some sort of imaginative balance.[71] This is one of the things that Iago *is*: an imaginative device for making visible something in the operation of time.

And as with time so it may be with realistic psychology. Liberties are taken with it—but not in the interest of sensation, or of such a fanciful invention as may please for a while. In *Othello* it is conceivable that the psychological integrity of the characters is in places weakened rather as Stoll avers, but by an imaginative power working to ends Stoll does not envisage. In this perhaps lies a solution of the difficulties we face.

That men do project upon others feelings and impulses which they would disavow is a fact obscurely known to us all, and I do not doubt its entering, in some measure, into our experience of *Othello*, with a consequent credibilising of Iago and his power.

But we are most of us more aware of the simpler and prior fact of our divided soul, of danger when our blood begins our safer guides to rule, of the conflict of passion and reason—self-division's cause. *Othello* is about this conflict. The core of the play is not this character or that but a love-relationship, and in this relationship passion and reason become suspicion and trust. Desdemona *is* trust and Othello *is* suspicion; we shall etiolate, and not strengthen, Shakespeare's "psychology" if we ignore this element of symbolism in the tragedy. When Granville-Barker declares

> The problem, then, and the essential structure of the play, will be psychological, the action primarily an interior action . . . in no other that he wrote does the immediate operation of mind upon mind count for so much—[72]

we must make this qualification: that the display of this operation of mind upon mind is still subsumed within an action essentially symbolical. The minds are, in some degree, the minds of abstractions. As Desdemona *is* trust and Othello *is* suspicion, so—strangely—Othello *is* the human soul as it strives to be and Iago *is* that which corrodes or subverts it from within. We have evolved a view of the play which renders plausible the mechanism of the "calumniator believed" in terms of modern mental science; and this, I say, is in the tragedy—which in this aspect remains a work of subtle but sufficient naturalism. But this is knit to—I judge is subsidiary to—an aspect in which the play is of imaginative rather than naturalistic articulation. And, in point of the chosen theme, the method is more dramatic, better theatre, and much more apt for a strong and pristine art.

I conjecture, then, that at certain cardinal moments in the play when poetically received Othello and Iago are felt less as individuals each with his own psychological integrity than as abstractions from a single and, as it were, invisible protagonist. There are expressive forms of drama in which we do patently see a man at grips with some externalised facet of himself; in *King Lear* there is perhaps momentarily something of the sort as between Lear himself and the Fool; and this is something familiar to us too in ballet, which is an essence of drama. There is a poetic form—almost a major form—in which much the same thing is rendered in terms of a dialogue between Self and Soul.

And something like this I see in the third Act of *Othello*: a realising of the basic mechanisms of the "calumniator believed" not naturalistically but through such an imaginative "splitting" as myth and poetry often employ to express violent polarities and ambivalences in the mind. The true protagonist of the drama (at least at this point) is to be arrived at only, as it were, by conflating two characters; by considering them (rather I should say by intuitively apprehending them) as interlocked forces within a single psyche. It is less a matter of Othello's projecting concealed facets of himself upon an apt Iago (a fundamentally naturalistic handling, such as is offered to us by Miss Maud Bodkin) than of the dramatist's abstracting these facets and embodying them in a figure substantially symbolic. Entailed in this is the view that Othello too is, at times, a figure substantially symbolic.

This hypothesis, I believe, will reconcile much in Stoll (his insistence upon Othello and Iago as not, individually regarded and at a crisis, sufficient and complete personalities) with much in Bradley (both his basic insistence upon the *truth* of the play, its powerful grasp of vehement real life, and upon the essential impression of the nobility of Othello as he appears before us). Again and again one writer whom I have cited jeers at the hopeless naïvety of Bradley in accepting as the *real* Othello what is no more than *Othello*'s Othello. But if we regard the Othello-figure on the stage as being indeed something in the nature of an Othello *persona*, as Othello's ego-ideal or self-exemplar, then Bradley is really right in point of dramatic feeling, since what we have here, in the sort of Soul-and-Body debate which the play essentially is, is indeed the "noble" Othello imaginatively disengaged, though far from immune, from the lower Othello, the Othello who has been externalised in (rather than merely projected upon) Iago.

Shakespeare's characters—this character and that character—often have far more "psychology" than historical realism would suppose. And, in so far as this holds, Shakespeare's drama is naturalistic in a simple, if not in the simplest, signification: it gives individuals as a profoundly intuitive mind is aware of them. But perhaps none of Shakespeare's great plays is merely naturalistic in this sense; and he does freely use characters like Iago who have at times, and as independent beings, no more psychology than Stoll is prepared to allow them. Nevertheless these characters are composed into a whole which, I think, has psychology, or which is in the total impression an image of life. Iago is unreal, and Stoll is right about him. Othello is unreal, and Stoll is right about him also. But the two together and in interaction are not unreal. The two together make your mind, or mine.

CHAPTER VI

THE BIRTH AND DEATH OF FALSTAFF

So well hath Shakespeare expressed all sorts of persons as one would think he had been transformed into every one of those he hath described. . . . Who would not think he had been such a man as Sir John Falstaff?

MARGARET, DUCHESS OF NEWCASTLE (1624?–1674)

IN dramatising the material of *1 & 2 Henry IV* and *Henry V* Shakespeare did not start entirely from scratch. We know almost nothing except this bare fact. *The Famous Victories,* or something very like it, may have been his "source," but it is possible that he worked from an earlier and fuller play of which *The Famous Victories* is a vestigial version.[73] When he created Sir John Falstaff, therefore, it is impossible to say whether he had before him anything more full-bodied than the shadowy comic material in the old play preserved to us. Nor can we tell whether he returned to his own text and revised it in the light of his maturing comic genius. Thus of what may be termed the gestation of Falstaff, and of his delivery whether lenitive or hard, only conjecture speaks. If his mother, when she looked down one three of the clock in the afternoon upon that white head and something round belly, murmured

Where do you come from, baby dear?—

she was only anticipating the question of many learned men on what dark night of forebeing first formed Sir John. Where does Falstaff come from? This is the grand problem of Falstaff's *birth* which Maurice Morgann really raised in the eighteenth century when he wrote an essay (he says) "professing to treat of the Courage of *Falstaff*, but extending itself to his Whole character." There is another problem, that of Falstaff's *death*, which the nineteenth century first became aware of. Some examination of critical approaches to these two problems will occupy this final chapter.

III

I

And first there is the view—to be mentioned only briefly—that Falstaff had his birth in what is nowadays called a "documentary"; that he is the offspring of a devoted social historian. This is maintained by Mr. John W. Draper, who holds that Shakespeare "aimed merely to depict men and things as they are," and then draws the hazardous inference that it was therefore his sufficient business to depict them as they stood sorted and categorised in the Elizabethan social consciousness.[74] Here, I think, is a modified form of the old doctrine of *decorum* in imaginative literature. Shakespeare's characters, it seems, must stand or fall according as they do or do not correctly embody the various traits proper to certain sorts of Elizabethan person. Research will show that they do this better than might casually be supposed. Research therefore enjoys the pleasant consciousness of backing Shakespeare up. And as Falstaff is "an essentially realistic creation," and clearly intended to appear as an army officer,

> logically then, one should study his character as an army officer, rather than in any other group of Elizabethan society. . . . Army life was on a very low plane.

When one has made this study one will *expect* Falstaff to frequent disreputable people and places, pawn his military equipment, lead his men to slaughter in order to steal their "dead pay"—and so forth. One may also learn something of the probable attitude of the audience to the various aspects of Falstaff's depravity. Some of his later activities (those which critics have seen as more heinous and designed increasingly to stress the shadier side of the character) the audience would be disposed to condone. But his early behaviour at Gadshill they would wholly condemn—for does not Digges in his *Paradoxes* declare that "cowardize in Man (especially professing Armes) hath ever been accounted the foulest vice"? Here, then, is a pointer to how the audience regarded Sir John: "recognising him as a common type in the London of the day, they surely could not quite suspend the feelings and judgments that they associated with the living examples."

But this sort of criticism, I fear, takes us nowhere on the road we would go. If we are really concerned a little to account for Falstaff, if we would descry some shadow of answer to the question "Where does he come from?" we shall certainly find little help in Mr. Draper's approach, since the quality of what Shakespeare offers (and it is this alone that tempts us to any inquiry at all) is left out of account. Explanations must be something adequate to what is explained. But a patent inadequacy, as here, may put us on guard in more colourable places.

There is another view of Falstaff's engendering—a very compendious one—which may be mentioned before coming to substantial matters. Nothing was involved in the event except what gynaecologists call (I have been told) a pseudocyesis; nothing so indelicate as Falstaff's birth ever really occurred. Here we have the belief of the New Bowdlers, whom man delights not, no, nor woman neither, and who would give us not merely *Hamlet* without the Prince but the Complete Works without their several *dramatis personae*. "Falstaff," says Mr. L. C. Knights, "is not a man, but a choric commentary."[75] Conceivably he is both. But before a statement so exclusive we must take ground with the common reader, who knows that Falstaff is a substantial citizen of a world thronged with men and women—men and women, doubtless, who are not as we are; but the nature of whose reality would tax metaphysical disquisition. It has taxed the scholastic mind of Professor Stoll.

2

Stoll approaches Falstaff as a genealogist and a determinist, convinced that the man's path was laid down at his nativity. "Capitano Spavento," Stoll says to those curious about the knight's ancestry, "Spezzafer, Fracasso, Matamoros, Spezza-Monti, Giangurgolo, Vappo, Rogantino."[76] It sounds magnificent enough—a lineage which, armorially translated, should make a fine showing on that seal-ring of his grandfather's which Sir John always carried. Alas! these sounding names belong, it seems, to a line more ancient than honourable, one prominent in men's eyes since clowns first grinned through horse-collars or tumbled on a plank. Falstaff descends from the poltroons of literature, from the rascally bragging soldiers of Roman comedy, and he is bound hand and foot by his heredity. We know his ancestors and therefore we can predict his *Lebenstil*—his life-style, since this is determined by these. He cannot be other than cowardly, much as a Hapsburg cannot have other than such a lip and such a chin. For always the nurture which the individual artist brings to his creations is of small account compared with the nature which they derive from literary convention. In framing Falstaff Shakespeare preserves "immemorial custom," "the established *lazzi* of the coward on the stage . . . not in England only but in contemporary Germany, Spain, and Italy," "the traditional comic situation," "all the conventional and traditional tricks of cowardice." Shakespeare had neither impulse nor need to do otherwise, since this submitting to convention strengthens the artist and enables him to concentrate upon that refinement within it which is his proper business:

> In the same period a great popular artist and a mediocre one use much the same means of expression—"business," situations and types. That is to say, the difference is in the touch.

And it is not in a psychological touch:

> Falstaff boasting and lying is treated typically, externally, . . . that he who chatters and scuffles in the pit may laugh and not fail.

Shakespeare was too conservative for *psychological* refinement—and this makes cobweb of most modern criticism of Falstaff.

> In real life both Sir Johns [Oldcastle and Fastolf] were brave and worthy fellows; they are thus overwhelmed with obloquy because in the popular imagination one charge, as this of heresy or that of cowardice, brings every other in its trail; but all that concerns us here is that in Shakespeare they are cowards because they were that before. Always our poet stands by public opinion, and his English kings or Roman heroes are to him what they were to his age.

But do we, perhaps, find in Shakespeare what we seek? Stoll's quest—his nose, we might say—is for "a convention, a bit of stage language . . . precise and ascertainable." His Shakespeare accordingly is above all things skilled in and subdued to "the stage language of his time—all the traditions and associations of ideas"; Shakespeare is little more than midwife to a fresh brood

of these. The learning of Mr. Stoll has enabled him to compre-
hend vividly the great theme of the continuity of literature, and
his satisfaction in discerning the ordering finger of the centuries
pointing Shakespeare his way has at times a quality almost
enthusiastic and mystical. Why did Shakespeare write *The Merry
Wives of Windsor?* Because, the legend has it, the Queen called
for a play of Sir John Falstaff in love and Shakespeare, taking the
luckless command in the only possible way, dashed off a capital
farce in a fortnight. For Stoll, however, the old legend will not
do.

> The figure of the braggart captain, which came into Shake-
> speare's hands from Plautus or from the Comedy of Masks, would
> have been incomplete if he had not appeared as the suitor gulled.

Is Falstaff, then, thus cramped in the buck-basket of a severe
literary determinism, simply a braggart captain paper-thin, and
nothing more? Stoll is far from saying this. "Falstaff . . . is not
an ordinary stage coward," he declares. Then in what does his
distinction lie? Wherein *does* consist that "difference . . . in the
touch"?

It is not, it seems, that Falstaff rises to any imperishable high
comedy. Humour like his, picaresque humour, "morals and
sentiments alike, in the lapse of time, obliterate." Either we must
submit to a historical discipline and endeavour to arrive at
Elizabethan notions of what is funny or we must submit to a
"process of critical emasculation"—joining those who, "because
of the tradition that he [Falstaff] is the supreme comic figure . . .
have endeavoured and laboured to like him," or rather to like a
sentimentalised substitute with a humorous constitution consonant with the manners of our time. Nevertheless Stoll must
face the fact that Falstaff is a person of status in English dramatic
history; that wherever cultivated people speak of Don Quixote
and Panurge they are likely to speak of Falstaff too; that the
knight is, in very fact, "Sir *Iohn* with all Europe." How is this
to be accounted for?

It is the language, Stoll says; and it is here that we shall find
an element really original to Shakespeare. What in Falstaff's
appeal is immediate and perpetual

> lies not so much in his conduct as in his speech. He talks
> prose but is supremely poetic, and his is in many ways the most

marvellous prose ever penned. It pulses with his vast vitality and irrepressible spirit, it glows with the warmth of his friendliness and good humour.

Now, this will hardly do. Falstaff, we have been told, is a stage coward, "treated typically, externally"; he is this redeemed by speech conceived as a magnificent garment concealing the stereotype within. But now (and in much more that Stoll finally says of "the magnetism of a personality," "the very spirit of comradeship," "the genius of converse") we are offered this great voice, this golden language as *expressing* personal qualities which the character may not, according to the hypothesis, *possess*. And here, it seems to me, is the central weakness of all Professor Stoll's criticism: it altogether misapprehends the creative situation; what is happening in the poet's mind when great voices begin to speak. Of course the poet uses language with a vast conscious craft to illustrate and adorn his conception. But just as, in poetry, the subtlety of the rhythm *is* the clarity of the emotion so, in drama, the voice *is* the character. We cannot penetrate through some rhetorical artifice in Falstaff to a spindle-shanked Capitano Spavento within, or catch him off guard, his wonderful speech hung

> loose about him, like a Giants Robe
> Upon a dwarfish Theefe.

Falstaff is something more than a dummy superlatively clothed, and Professor Stoll's theory of his birth is inadequate just as Mr. Draper's theory is inadequate, if less patently so. In Stoll's paper we are nowhere with Falstaff and nowhere with Shakespeare; we are with a Shakespeare from whom a specific creative power has been withdrawn. It is otherwise with Maurice Morgann's famous essay. This essay brings us close to Shakespeare. Or so I feel. And what I want to do now is to account to myself for this feeling. What makes this government official's whimsical defence of Falstaff's valour one of the great places in the criticism of Shakespeare?

Morgann, like Sir Max Beerbohm's Matthew Arnold, was not always wholly serious. He tells us that he "has endeavoured to preserve to his Text a certain lightness of air, and cheerfulness of tone," and moreover confesses himself "unengaged"—meaning thereby that he was among those "idle and unemployed" who were the most likely, according to the contemporary aesthetic, to take a fanciful view of things. Morgann's view of Falstaff is in aspects undeniably fanciful; it could hardly be otherwise since he sets out frankly in quest of literary diversion and defends his chosen paradox of Falstaff's constitutional courage with arguments which sometimes have only ingenuity and charm to recommend them. The vein of *bagatelle* which runs through the *Essay on the Dramatic Character of Sir John Falstaff* may prevent our acknowledging its essence: an understanding of where great dramatic creations have their birth.[77]

3

Morgann's foible is notorious: in his imagination he sees Falstaff as something very close to a historical personage. He discusses his off-stage activities, the fugitive and unexpressed impulses of his mind, the influences to which he would be exposed in boyhood as page to Thomas Mowbray, his lineage as it may be conjectured from scattered hints in the drama— inferring the *a priori* likelihood of his courage from "the circumstances and condition of his whole life and character." Thus:

> We discover ... that in a very early period of his life he was familiar with *John* of *Gaunt*; which could hardly be, unless he had possessed much personal gallantry and accomplishment, and had derived his birth from a distinguished at least, if not from a Noble family. ... It is observable that Courage is a quality which is at least as transmissible to one's posterity as features and complexion. In these periods men acquired and maintained their rank and possessions by personal prowess and gallantry; and their marriage alliances were made, of course, in families of the same character. ... It is not therefore beside my purpose to inquire what hints of the origin and birth of *Falstaff*, *Shakespeare* may have dropped in different parts of the Play; for tho' we may be disposed to allow that *Falstaff* in his old age might, under particular influences, desert the point of honour, we cannot give up that unalienable possession of Courage, which might have been derived to him from a noble or distinguished stock.

Can this seemingly wayward manner of going to work be

defended? It is plain that Morgann believes so, and that his thesis deliberately blends paradox and sober critical statement.

> There is a certain roundness and integrity in the forms of *Shakespeare*, which give them an independence as well as a relation, insomuch that we often meet with passages which, tho' perfectly felt, cannot be sufficiently explained in words, without unfolding the whole character of the speaker. . . . The reader will not now be surprised if I affirm that those characters in *Shakespeare*, which are seen only in part, are yet capable of being unfolded and understood in the whole; every part being in fact relative, and inferring all the rest.

In other words it is permissible to consider Shakespeare's characters

> rather as Historic than Dramatic beings; and, when occasion requires, to account for their conduct from the *whole* of character, from general principles, from latent motives, and from policies not avowed.

In Shakespeare's characters, then, we are aware, just as we are in actual people, of depths and facets not immediately rendered in behaviour. They seem to carry about with them a fuller and more complex humanity than is required by the exigencies of their rôle. It is this that makes them so lifelike, and our intuitive apprehension of the *whole* character is an important part of our experience of the play. At first the understanding pronounces Falstaff to be indeed a coward—the mere braggart soldier Stoll sees. But at the same time we are aware that Shakespeare "has contrived to make secret Impressions upon us of Courage." And if we respect these impressions, if we treat them as a trained historian might treat his underlying sense of some historical portrait's being as yet incomplete, if we work by inference from what is overt to what is concealed—if we do this we shall eventually vindicate our intuition before the bar of the understanding, and appreciate that the entire artistry in Shakespeare's creation of Falstaff consists in the disparity between the real or whole character (which is courageous) and the partial or apparent character (which is cowardly). It is as if we worked from a few bones which had immediately suggested themselves as those of a common rooster, and were presently delightfully confirmed in an always present intuition that here was an altogether rarer fowl.

And indeed it might be possible to draw some defence of Morgann's method from the biological sciences, and particularly from the work of Georges Cuvier, who was eight years old when the *Essay* was published. "Every part being in fact relative, and inferring all the rest." Morgann's perception here is precisely of that principle of the "correlation of parts" with which Cuvier too pursued rare fowl—as will sufficiently appear in the following quotation from a standard history of science:

> Organs do not exist or function separately in nature, but only as parts of complete living things. In these living things certain relations are observed which are fundamental to their mode of life. Thus feathers are always found in birds, and never in other creatures. The presence of feathers is related to a certain formation of the forelimb, with reference to its action as wing. . . . But the wing-structure . . . is in turn related to certain formations of the collar-bone and breast-bone, with reference to the function of flight; these, again, to the form and movement of the chest. . . . Thus, given a feather, it is possible to infer that its owner had a particular form of collar-bone, a particular kind of skeleton, a particular type of mouth. . . . In Cuvier's hands the principle of correlation could often be brought to bear upon the merest fragment. From a little bit of leg bone, for example, even the "leggy" nature of which no one but a trained naturalist could guess, he succeeded in reconstructing an entire giant bird of a very aberrant type. His reconstruction was proved to be accurate by subsequent discoveries.[78]

Morgann's reconstructed Falstaff too is a "giant bird"—and for one of Stoll's thinking a type so aberrant as to be unbelievable. And alas! here there seems no possible check through actual discovery. When Cuvier meditated his leggy fragment specimens of the whole creature did lurk in the rocks. He was reasoning towards something actual. But Sir John was alone the Arabian bird; his only bones are gone to dust in Eastcheap; and nowhere does his fellow lie. A play—it may be declared by way of dismissing Morgann—is an artifice, not a document or historical record. And to suggest that we may work towards an actual whole by inference from the parts which alone have ever existed is merely whimsical. For the characters in a play, Shakespeare's as another's, have no being except as they, or the illusions of them, are conjured up before us by print on a page or by actors mouthing before a scene.

But is this manner of having done with Maurice Morgann and his haunting sense of some fuller being behind the outline on the stage (for that is the essence of his feeling) justifiable? Or is there really a "giant bird"? Are the ways of the imagination indeed such that dramatic characters can partake of some larger life—a life of which only "secret impressions" are yielded in the theatre?

I think there is a sense in which we can, in fact, say of Shakespeare's great characters that "the parts which are not seen do ... exist." An intuitive understanding of the processes of dramatic creation lies beneath the "lightness of air" of Morgann's *Essay* and makes it memorable as Shakespeare criticism.

4

Why does a man write plays or novels, after all; and how does he possess himself of the people who feel and act in them? On this Morgann himself has something to say—not much, but sufficient to set us on our road:

> But it was not enough for *Shakespeare* to have formed his characters with the most perfect truth and coherence; it was further necessary that he should possess a wonderful facility of compressing, as it were, his own spirit into these images, and of giving alternate animation to the forms. This was not to be done *from without*; he must have *felt* every varied situation, and have spoken thro' the organ he had formed. Such an intuitive comprehension of things and such a facility must unite to produce a *Shakespeare*. ... The characters of *Shakespeare* are thus *whole*, and as it were original.

"Compressing, as it were, his own spirit into these images." Coleridge, Morgann's immediate successor in the great line of Shakespeare critics—and another who believed that "Shakespeare's characters are like those in life, to be *inferred* by the reader"—takes us further when he notes

> Shakespeare's mode of conceiving characters out of his own intellectual and moral faculties, by conceiving any one intellectual or moral faculty in morbid excess and then placing himself, thus mutilated and diseased, under given circumstances.[79]

Coleridge's words here take colouring from their being directed at an elucidation of the character of Hamlet, but the perception underlying them is clear. The artist does not get the essence of his characters from camera-work, as Mr. Draper would suppose; nor yet from a filing-cabinet of traditional literary types, which is the belief Professor Stoll constantly expresses with what softening word he can. He gets his characters from an interplay of these with something inside. And it is because he has a particular sort of inside, or psychic constitution, that he is obliged to get them. Falstaff and his peers are the product of an imagination working urgently from within. The sum of the characters is a sort of sum—nay, gives something like the portrait—of Shakespeare: a truth which Walter Bagehot realises in his essay, *Shakespeare—the Man*.[80] ("If anybody could have any doubt about the liveliness of Shakespeare, let him consider the character of Falstaff.") But we do not quite express the matter by saying (what is obvious enough) that Shakespeare had immense perceptive and apperceptive power; that he could recognise in himself all the elements variously combined in the motley humanity about him, and so draw, with an original authority, the characters of many men and many women. To this we must add that there is typically in the artist an instability; a reluctance of elements, in themselves abnormally numerous, available and potent, to combine hierarchically in the formation of one permanent character; a corresponding impulse to build up now one and now another impermanent configuration of traits. "Now Master up, now Miss"—said Pope, projecting an extreme of this constitution upon his enemy. And here too is what Keats recognised as the chameleon nature of the poet.[81]

The inquiries of James and others into the phenomena of conversion, and of later investigators in the field of multiple and split personality (did Falstaff indeed have a Dr. Jekyll who drove the common tenement of clay hoarse with halloing and singing of anthems?) have shown how, in abnormal individuals not artistically endowed, either a co-presence or a succession of perfectly "real" personalities can be a psychological fact. And a man writes plays or novels, I conceive, partly at least because he is beset by unexpressed selves; by the subliminal falling now into one coherent pattern and now into another of the varied elements of his total man—elements many of which will never, except in his writing, find play in consciousness.[82] It is this that gives the characters their "independence as well as relation"; their

I

haunting suggestion of reality and of a larger, latent being unexhausted in the action immediately before us; their ability to beckon beyond the narrow limits of their hour. And here, too, we see how characters "come alive"—how Falstaff came alive. It was not that Shakespeare took a traditional figure and clothed it with the spurious animation of a dazzling dress. It was that he took that figure and infused into it as much—and only as much —of the Falstaff-being in himself as the exigencies of his design would admit. Of what more there was unused the bouquet, it may be, floats across the stage in those "secret impressions" which Morgann felt. And sherris and ambrosia mingle there.

We have discovered, I think, why Morgann's essay is so much nearer to Shakespeare than Stoll's. Morgann better understands being creative. Stoll sees Shakespeare making his book as Stoll would make a book: knowing just what he would do, assembling his material from all available sources, and then constructing according to the best professional specifications of his age. But Morgann knows that nothing was ever born alive this way, and that despite all the artist owes to tradition and convention his is an inner travail still. That he draws from tradition is assured, and he will be the better, perhaps, for having before him the idea of the literary kind to which he would contribute. But *what* he contributes will be his own, or nothing in art. It will be radically his own, and not an old thing resurfaced. For the essence of his task is in exploring an inward abundance. When he does this in drama his characters, sympathetically received, will inevitably suggest to us a life beyond the limits of their rôle. And Shakespeare, from the vast heaven of his mind, expresses whole constellations of emotion in personative form; it is nothing other than this that Morgann means when he asks:

> For what is *Falstaff*, what *Lear*, what *Hamlet*, or *Othello*, but different modifications of *Shakespeare's* thought?

5

Before the death of Falstaff comes what is commonly regarded as its precipitating cause, his rejection—which we shall find, however, not so much the cause of death as a death itself.

I know thee not, old man: Fall to thy Prayers:
How ill white haires become a Foole, and Iester!
I haue long dream'd of such a kinde of man,
So surfeit-swell'd, so old, and so prophane:
But being awake, I do despise my dreame.
Make lesse thy body (hence) and more thy Grace,
Leaue gourmandizing; Know the Graue doth gape
For thee, thrice wider than for other men.
Reply not to me, with a Foole-borne Iest . . .

It is uncomfortable reading—uncomfortable both in its extreme
dramatic subtlety, as of the transition to this last line from the
two lines preceding, and in its total effect:

Reply not to me, with a Foole-borne Iest,
Presume not, that I am the thing I was,
For heauen doth know (so shall the world perceiue)
That I haue turn'd away my former Selfe,
So will I those that kept me Companie.
When thou dost heare I am, as I haue bin,
Approach me, and thou shalt be as thou was't
The Tutor and the Feeder of my Riots:
Till then, I banish thee, on paine of death,
As I haue done the rest of my Misleaders,
Not to come neere our Person, by ten mile.
For competence of life, I will allow you,
That lacke of meanes enforce you not to euill:
And as we heare you do reforme your selues,
We will according to your strength, and qualities,
Giue you aduancement. Be it your charge (my Lord)
To see perform'd the tenure of our word. Set on.

It is much more uncomfortable than the corresponding speech in
the "old play" preserved to us as *The Famous Victories*:

Hen. 5. I prethee Ned, mend thy maners,
And be more modester in thy tearmes,
For my vnfeined greefe is not to be ruled by thy flattering
And dissembling talke, thou saist I am changed,
So I am indeed, and so must thou be, and that quickly,
Or else I must cause thee to be chaunged.
Ioc. Gogs wounds how like yo this?
Sownds tis not so sweete as Musicke.
Tom. I trust we haue not offended your grace no way.
Hen. 5. Ah *Tom*, your former life greeues me,

> And makes me to abandon & abolish your company for euer
> By ten miles space, then if I heare wel of you,
> It may be I wil do somewhat for you,
> Otherwise looke for no more fauour at my hands,
> Then at any other mans: And therefore be gone,
> We haue other matters to talke on.

Tolstoy found the old *King Leir* at least less bad than Shakespeare's play;[83] and here, in the deal of skimble-skamble stuff that makes up *The Famous Victories*, is something more decent and subdued than Shakespeare's version. But it is something, of course, immensely less effective. The first thing to note is that, in this rejection, Shakespeare pulls out all the stops of his instrument. It is a resounding *coda*, the discovery and anatomy of which as a *problem* makes one of the curious chapters in modern Shakespeare criticism.

6

Were we to pursue this problem about our university cities to-day we should encounter a remarkable successiono f conflicting voices, and this particularly in the crucial matter of Prince Henry's character and motive. At Oxford, or in its environs, we might meet the Poet Laureate, who has declared that

> Prince Henry is not a hero, he is not a thinker, he is not even a friend; he is a common man whose incapacity for feeling enables him to change his habits whenever interest bids him. Throughout the first acts he is careless and callous, though he is breaking his father's heart and endangering his father's throne. . . . He impresses one as quite common, quite selfish, quite without feeling. When he learns that his behaviour may have lost him his prospective crown, he passes a sponge over his past and fights like a wildcat for the right of not having to work for a living.[84]

Were we to move to Edinburgh we might hear Professor Dover Wilson, incomparable Sherlock Holmes among Shakespeare's editors, liken this same young prince to Spenser's Red Cross Knight, declare his regeneration to be "reasonable and human," his character "the soul of true honour," the manner of Falstaff's rejection "a happy solution," his committal to the Fleet "even something of a compliment," and any opinions maintained to the contrary to-day to be "characteristically muddle-headed."[85] Were we next to travel south to Manchester we might be admitted to the lecture-room of Professor Charlton, who finds in the rejection not a happy solution but the issue of "cumulative priggishness" and "callous cruelty" after which it is "unthinkable that our feelings towards [Prince Hal] can remain sympathetically genial." "It seems a safe guess that such a Hal, so false to Falstaff, will of that seed grow to a greater falseness. If indeed, a greater falseness is within the scope of conjecture."[86]

So much for the soul of true honour and for the Red Cross Knight. In London we could, unhappily, no longer hear a voice which some fifteen years ago told us that Hal is "the kind of personality that can no more be smircht by circumstance than white-hot iron by dust"; nor in Cambridge one which on the contrary roundly declared Hal's rejection of Falstaff to be suspiciously synchronous with Shakespeare's preparing to leave London, buying property in Stratford and generally turning respectable.[87] And Quiller-Couch pointed, as many critics have done, to a root of our discomforts in Hal's soliloquy at the close of *1 Henry IV*, Act I, ii. "I know you all," Hal says, when Falstaff, Poins and the rest have gone out—

> I know you all, and wil a while vphold
> The vnyokt humour of your idlenes,
> Yet herein wil I imitate the sunne,
> Who doth permit the base contagious clouds
> To smother vp his beauties from the world,
> That when he please againe to be himselfe,
> Being wanted he may be more wondred at . . .

"The most damnable piece of workmanship to be found in any of his plays," Quiller-Couch declares of this speech, and continues:

> This, if we accept it, poisons what follows, poisons the madcap Prince in our imagination for good and all. Most of us can forgive youth, hot blood, riot: but a prig of a rake, rioting on a calculated scale, confessing that he does it coldly, intellectually, and that he proposes to desert his comrades at the right moment to better his own repute—*that* kind of rake surely all honest men abhor. . . .
> We cannot keep them [the lines of the soliloquy] and keep any opinion of Henry as a decent fellow. . . . Falstaff had never consciously hurt Henry, had never—so far from unkindness—thought

of him but kindly. Wisely or not—wisely, if we will—Henry had hurt Falstaff to death: and not for any *new* default, sin or crime, but for continuing to be, in fault and foible, the very same man in whose faults and foibles he had delighted as a friend.

Then, if the object of the new play be—as all will admit—to present King Harry as our patriotic darling, henceforth Bates and Williams are good enough for him to practise his talk upon, and he may rant about St. Crispin's Day until the lowing herd winds slowly o'er the lea. But he must not be allowed to meet Falstaff. As he once very prettily said of Hotspur—

> Two stars keep not their motion in one sphere

and therefore he must not be allowed to meet Falstaff. *For Falstaff can kill him with a look.*

This advances beyond the rejection to an explanation of the death; at the same time it very fairly represents the majority opinion of modern critics, whether muddle-headed or not. Thus if we were to make another foray across the Border and arrive at Glasgow we should find Professor Alexander holding that if Hal's soliloquy is to be regarded as in full dramatic keeping and revelatory of a detached and self-controlled nature then the man who speaks it has no right "to turn without warning on his companions, when it suits him to cast them off, and to point to Falstaff as 'the tutor and the feeder of my riots.' "[88] The conclusion here is that Hal "is not the offspring of the poet's reflection and passion"—from which it would follow (I suppose) that in his trilogy Shakespeare was not very profoundly concerned with working towards an ideal kingship. But at Cambridge again—and finally—we should find Mr. E. M. W. Tillyard declaring the Prince to be indeed Shakespeare's attempt at defining the perfect ruler. And if we incline to sympathise with so dangerous a rebel as Falstaff we are being misled by "the sense of security created in nineteenth-century England by the predominance of the British navy."[89]

7

The little tour we have just concluded should at least give us the main terms of the problem, a problem adumbrated by Nicholas Rowe in 1709 when he wrote of Falstaff:

[Shakespeare] has given him so much Wit as to make him almost too agreeable; and I don't know whether some People have not, in remembrance of the Diversion he had formerly afforded 'em, been sorry to see his Friend *Hal* use him so scurvily, when he comes to the Crown in the End of the Second Part of *Henry* the Fourth.[90]

The "scurvy" treatment of Falstaff is quite in keeping with a certain insensibility in the Elizabethans which appears in many gulling scenes on the stage. But we are liable to feel it not consonant either with Shakespeare's humanity to a major creation, or with the sympathy and admiration which must surely be claimed from us for Hal, a character who is being "groomed" (as the studios say) for the field of Agincourt. We may now consider more at large certain efforts at a solution of the problem.

Can we find some light in which the rejection of Falstaff commends itself to our sympathies while operating wholly within the sphere of psychological realism? I must say in advance that I think the answer to be "No." All through the trilogy there are penetrations enough into a deeper Harry Monmouth, and the rejection can be analysed in terms of these. But, by and large, I think something profounder is operating here than Shakespeare's understanding of the son of Henry Bolingbroke. There are times in all drama when immemorial forces come into play, and with the end of Falstaff we touch once more what Professor Schücking is fond of calling the limits of Shakespearian realism.

In terms of essential drama Falstaff's rejection and death are very important—indeed they are the end of the whole business. Falstaff's corner of *Henry V* is extremely haunting; the rest is a slack-water play, stirred here and there by simple patriotic feeling. For comedy now Shakespeare had so little list that he fell back upon comic Scots, Irish and Welshmen—the resource, I think I may say, of a professional entertainer hard pressed indeed. Moreover, that the poet of *Romeo and Juliet* should have executed the wooing of Katharine—that *ne plus ultra* of all obtuseness—must fill us with dismay until we persuade ourselves (with a school of critics romantic, no doubt) that there here glints at us from behind the mask the master's most inscrutable smile. In a word, all this matter ends for Shakespeare with Falstaff and not with a foreign conquest; and there must be reason for this.

8

And first there is Bradley, whose acknowledgment of the uncomfortableness of the rejection is emphatic.[91] If we have enjoyed the Falstaff scenes (and Shakespeare surely meant them to be enjoyed), we feel a good deal of pain and some resentment when Henry first turns upon his old companion with talk like a clergyman's and then sends back the Chief Justice to commit him to prison; nor are our regrets diminished when, in *Henry V*, it is powerfully suggested to us that Falstaff has, in fact, died of wounded affection. Why did Shakespeare end his drama with a scene which, though undoubtedly striking, leaves an impression so unpleasant?

What troubles us is not only the disappointment of Falstaff—it is the conduct of Henry. Shakespeare might surely have so arranged the matter that "the King could have communicated his decision, and Falstaff could have accepted it, in a private interview rich in humour and merely touched with pathos." Instead, we are given something both ungenerous and insincere —for with what colour can this strong and independent prince, whose wildness (or appearance of it) has by his own confession been matter of deliberate policy, speak either of Falstaff as the tutor and the feeder of his riots, or of Falstaff's inconsiderable followers as his misleaders? Part, surely, of the explanation of our discomfort must be this: that we have misread both the Prince's character and Shakespeare's attitude to character in general. We conventionalise Shakespeare by expecting him to mark his approval or disapproval of characters, and even by expecting him to divide them into simple sheep and goats; if he is impartial he disconcerts us; if he does *not* make sign of disapproval we neglect the possibility of his nevertheless disapproving—and so we blame him for indifference. And in this particular place:

> Our fault lies not in our resentment at Henry's conduct but in our surprise at it; ... if we had read his character truly in the light that Shakespeare gave us, we should have been prepared for a display both of hardness and of policy at this point in his career[92].

Both as prince and as king Henry is deservedly a favourite, but a strong strain of policy has been evident in him from the first, as has an incapacity for any warmth of personal relations outside his own family. Thus his conduct in rejecting Falstaff proves on scrutiny to be in perfect keeping with his character on its unpleasant side, as well as on that finer side which leads him to dedicate himself to kingship.

But all this—Bradley continues—will not solve the problem. For we are left supposing that Shakespeare *intended* us to feel resentment against Henry, and this cannot be. It follows that he must have designed our sympathy with Falstaff to be so far weakened that we should accept the rejection and pass lightly over that disclosure of unpleasant traits in the King's character which the poet's artistry would not let him suppress. The conclusion of this part of the argument is clear:

> Thus our pain and resentment, if we feel them, are wrong, in the sense that they do not answer to the dramatist's intention. But it does not follow that they are wrong in a further sense. They may be right, because the dramatist has missed what he aimed at. And this, though the dramatist was Shakespeare, is what I would suggest. In the Falstaff scenes he overshot his mark. He created so extraordinary a being, and fixed him so firmly on his intellectual throne, that when he sought to dethrone him he could not. The moment comes when we are to look at Falstaff in a serious light, and the comic hero is to figure as a baffled schemer; but we cannot make the required change, either in our attitude or in our sympathies.

So in what, we are now asked, essentially consists Falstaff's indefeasible attractiveness? The bliss of freedom gained in humour is the essence of him. He denies that life is real or life is earnest, and delivers us from the oppression of such nightmares, and lifts us into an atmosphere of perfect freedom—as for example when he maintains untouched, in the face of imminent peril and even when he *feels* the fear of death, the very same power of dissolving it in persiflage that he shows when he sits at ease in his inn. Again, his lies are not designed to win serious conviction; there is nothing serious in any of them except the refusal to take anything seriously. And again, his cowardice and running away are presented as the characteristics rather of one who has risen superior to all serious motives than of one who is, in the ordinary sense, a coward.

But although the main source, then, of our sympathetic delight in Falstaff is his humorous superiority to everything serious, and the freedom of soul enjoyed in it, yet this, of course, is not the whole of his character. His godlike freedom has consequences and conditions; he cannot eat and drink for ever without money; and so he is driven to evil deeds—and these in themselves make an ugly picture. Now, *Henry IV* was to be in the main a historical play, and its chief hero Prince Henry. Falstaff at last *must* be disgraced, and must therefore appear no longer as the invincible humorist, but as an object of ridicule and even of aversion. Shakespeare's purpose being thus to work a gradual change in our feelings towards him, and to tinge the humorous atmosphere more and more deeply with seriousness, we see him carrying out this purpose in the Second Part. Here he separates the Prince from Falstaff as much as he can, and exhibits more and more of the knight's seamy side: the heartless destroyer of Mrs. Quickly, the ruffian seriously defying the Chief Justice, the pike preparing to snap up the poor old dace Shallow, the worn-out lecher. Yet all this fails of its effect, and could have succeeded only had Shakespeare resigned himself to clouding over or debasing the humour of Falstaff. This he was too much of an artist to do, and so he does not succeed in changing our sympathy into repulsion. Shakespeare, in fact, was caught up on the wind of his own genius, and carried so far that he could not descend to earth at the selected spot. And yet the issue is not finally to be regretted very much:

> To show that Falstaff's freedom of soul was in part illusory, and that the realities of life refused to be conjured away by his humour —this was what we might expect from Shakespeare's unfailing sanity, but it was surely no achievement beyond the power of lesser men. The achievement was Falstaff himself, and the conception of that freedom of soul, a freedom illusory only in part, and attainable only by a mind which had received from Shakespeare's own the inexplicable touch of infinity which he bestowed on Hamlet and Macbeth and Cleopatra, but denied to Henry the Fifth.

9

There is so much of suggestion in Bradley's essay that more than one critic has found in it a starting-point for reflections of his own. Thus the germ of Professor Charlton's interpretation is essentially in the notion "that Falstaff's freedom of soul was in part illusory, and that the realities of life refused to be conjured away by his humour"—or in this and an earlier statement of Bradley's that, like no other Shakespearian character, "Falstaff was degraded by Shakespeare himself."

In *The Merry Wives of Windsor* Shakespeare, as it were, re-conventionalises Falstaff; turns him so decidedly into a gull and a buffoon that the thing is like a rejection in itself, or a manifesto of complete eventual disinterest in the character. Why does Shakespeare, even more cruelly than Henry, thus trample Falstaff into extinction? Because, Charlton says, Falstaff had let Shakespeare down. Falstaff revealed himself as being not what Shakespeare sought: an adequate comic hero, equipped for the true freedom of the world of comedy. And this letting Shakespeare down seems to have provoked a positive animus in the poet against his creation. Not only did it produce the "ruthless exposure, [the] almost malicious laceration" of the *Merry Wives*; it is the reason why Falstaff was not gently dismissed on some pre-coronation deathbed, but brutally in "a scene which has aroused more repugnance than any other in Shakespeare," and as a result of actions in Henry which are "an offence against humanity, and an offence which dramatically never becomes a skill."

What, then, according to this theory, is that true nature of a comic hero to which Falstaff fails to measure up? Since a comedy is a play which ends happily its hero, we are told, must be

likely to overcome whatever impediments to his well-being may be presented by the episodes of the play; and these episodes . . . must be representative of the obstacles which, in experience at large, are presented to man in the dilemmas inherent in more or less normal encounters with the world as the world is.

The comic hero, in fact, "must be endowed with the temperament and the arts to triumph over the stresses of circumstance." Now, Falstaff is insatiably curious to provide situations which test or even strain his genius for overcoming them. Mastery of circumstance is his pride—and so superficially he is an incomparable comic hero. But on a deeper view his attitude or philosophy is inadequate to cope with life even within that scope of worldly wisdom which is the philosophy of comedy. In the scene which a mature comedy must contemplate there are forces which Falstaff's measuring-stick cannot measure, and

> the world in which Falstaff's successors in comedy would have to prove their genius for mastery, would necessarily have to be a larger and a richer world than Falstaff's.

Hence Falstaff's failure, and Shakespeare's ruthless writing of him off.

If there is anything in the argument I have earlier advanced —to wit, that the major creations of a dramatist represent so many possible blendings or equilibriums of the abundant raw materials of personality which are his in virtue of his artist's nature—we must regard Charlton's argument as of considerable interest. But whatever be the dynamics of dramatic creation it would surely be extravagant to suggest that the artist's various progeny represent so many tentative essays in self-improvement —the bad shots among which he will then be prompted to "trample into extinction." For the dramatist is quite plainly not seeking about for an exemplar; rather he is like a pagan constructing a pantheon in which there shall be variously reflected the many sides of his own nature; and his satisfaction is simply in creation and in abundance. Thus such a psychological theory as I have hinted at affords no reason to suppose that Shakespeare would be particularly prone to turn upon Falstaff and disown or destroy him. If, on the other hand, we eschew psychology and stick to aesthetics, and with Charlton view Shakespeare's problem simply as one within the theory of comedy, we may believe indeed that Shakespeare might lose interest in Falstaff, but not that he would harry him. And it is just our sense of a persecution that has to be explained. Bradley's is still, perhaps, the best explanation: our having this sense results from Shakespeare's failing of his intention to manœuvre Falstaff into an unsympathetic light. But is there anything more to be said?

10

Obviously, one possibility remains. Shakespeare *succeeded* in manœuvring Falstaff into an unsympathetic light. If, with

Bradley, we feel otherwise, we are being sentimental, un-Elizabethan, and disregardful of the fortunes of Falstaff as the drama develops. This is the contention of Professor Dover Wilson.

That Shakespeare himself rejected Falstaff is nonsense, Dover Wilson says; in the Epilogue to *Henry IV* he promised more of him, and if, instead, *Henry V* gave an account of his death this was simply the best way of dealing with the awkward fact that Will Kempe, who created the part, had left the Lord Chamberlain's men. Thus all that falls to be considered is the propriety and dramatic fitness of Henry's dismissing Falstaff in the way he does. In discussing Falstaff, therefore, Dover Wilson would hold within the bounds of the two parts of *Henry IV*; and his case is that we should mark at once their unity and—more adequately than Bradley—their presentation of a Falstaff who by no means remains the same person throughout. His status changes. As a result of ludicrous deception, and quite without any deserving, he becomes a person of altogether more consideration than he was at first. This rise in his fortunes—from something like "the prince's jester," "an allowed fool" or a "rascally old camp-follower," to one generally supposed the vanquisher of Hotspur—discovers him to be arrogant and overweening; and these traits if they are not obscured to us do in fact alienate our sympathies. Moreover Shakespeare's dramatic intention is perfectly clear if we do not, like Bradley who ignores the serial character of dramatic representation, construct our own portrait of Falstaff almost entirely from the first part of the play. If we really *follow* the play we shall find that though Falstaff's wit grows no less fascinating he comes to inspire less and less affection. And this is enough to render the rejection palatable—always supposing that we remember another relevant fact, to the exposition of which Dover Wilson devotes much space. The story of the Prodigal Prince and his Misleader is, at a certain important level, a Morality. It is the Morality of a Ruler who has to make choice between Vanity and Government; it is "a Tudor version of a time-honoured theme," in which "the forces of iniquity were allowed full play upon the stage, including a good deal of horse-play, provided they were brought to nought, or safely locked up in Hell, at the end." So must not Falstaff, then, be locked up in the Fleet? The fact is that the Falstaff-Hal plot embodies a composite myth which had been centuries amaking, and was for the Elizabethans full of meaning that has largely disappeared since then. . . . They [the audience] knew, from the beginning, that the reign of this marvellous Lord of Misrule must have an end, that Falstaff must be rejected by the Prodigal Prince, when the time for reformation came. . . . Prince Hal and Falstaff, for us merely characters in a play, were for the Elizabethans that and a great deal more. They embodied in dramatic form a miscellaneous congeries of popular notions and associations, almost all since gone out of mind, in origin quasi-historical or legendary, pagan and Christian, ethical and political, theatrical, topographical and even gastronomic.

In other words, the Falstaff-Hal story subsumes divers traditional significances for the most part already embodied in drama, and the rejection scene is unexceptionable to an audience aware of and properly balancing these. Thus Falstaff partakes of the character not only of the *miles gloriosus* of Latin comedy, of the Devil of the Miracle Plays, of the Vice of the Moralities, of the traditional boon-companion of Henry, of the historical Oldcastle and Fastolfe; he partakes too of the character of Riot in the early Tudor interludes, and in one of these—*The Enterlude of Youth*—he is quite remarkably paralleled. This little play

opens with a dialogue between Youth and Charity. The young man, heir to his father's land, gives insolent expression to his self-confidence, lustihood, and contempt for spiritual things. Whereupon Charity leaves him, and he is joined by Riot, that is to say wantonness, who presently introduces him to Pride and Lechery. The dialogue then becomes boisterous, and continues in that vein for some time, much no doubt to the enjoyment of the audience. Yet, in the end, Charity reappears with Humility; Youth repents; and the interlude terminates in the most seemly fashion imaginable. . . .

Riot, like Falstaff, escapes from tight corners with a quick dexterity; like Falstaff, commits robbery on the highway; like Falstaff, jests immediately afterwards with his young friend on the subject of hanging; and like Falstaff, invites him to spend the stolen money at a tavern, where, he promises, "We will drink diuers wine" and "Thou shalt haue a wench to kysse Whansoeuer thou wilte"; allurements which prefigure the Boar's Head and Mistress Doll Tearsheet.

Riot, then, "prefigures" Falstaff, and the Tudor attitude to Riot must be taken into account when we come to consider the discomfiture of the knight.

What Dover Wilson is really providing here, it might be maintained, is a sort of second line of defence. As a person, or character in a drama realistically conceived, Falstaff is gradually so developed that we are not disturbed at seeing him turned off by another character carefully developed in terms of the same sort of realistic drama. But if we *are* disturbed we are to recall that this representation has a sort of abstract or allegorical quality as well, and fortify ourselves by considering "what would have followed had the Prince chosen Vanity instead of Government, Falstaff and not the Lord Chief Justice." Is this an illogical way of tackling the problem, arguing both for the psychological integrity of the drama and for an overriding myth which the characters must obey? It seems to me an explanation not much contrary to the logic of the theatre, where actions and situations have frequently more than one significance, and where these significances are often at an obscure interplay. Shakespeare's characters, I think, are nearly always real human beings before they are anything else; but undeniably they *are* at times something else: they take on the simpler rôles of archetypal drama; and then there will be "edges" (as the painters say) between generic character and psychological portraiture which the dramatist must cope with, using what finesse he can. It seems to me, therefore, that Dover Wilson gets furthest with the problem; and I am only concerned to wonder whether a further stone or two may yet be added to the edifice he has raised.

II

Two points would seem to be significant. If Shakespeare does indeed succeed in making the rejection palatable to persons adequately aware of traditional matters lying behind the play, it is yet in the theatre that he does so, for that the thing continues to *read* uncomfortably after all that Dover Wilson has to say I believe there will be few to deny. What does this mean? It means that although Shakespeare doubtless relied on certain contemporary attitudes to Riot and the like, he relied even more

on something perennially generated in the consciousness or disposition of an audience in a theatre—whether they belong to
Elizabethan times or to our own. And it is here that I would knit
the debate on Falstaff to the theme of the present book. For what
I have tried to urge is simply this: that in the interpretation of
Shakespeare a study of the psychology of poetic drama (which
leads us to understand his *medium*) is at least as important as a
study of the contemporary climate of opinion (which gives simply
conditions under which he worked).

The second point concerns the emphatic and wonderful
account in *Henry V* of the death of Falstaff. It is all very well for
Dover Wilson to point to the promise of more Falstaff made in
the Epilogue to *2 Henry IV* and infer that the subsequent death
was a matter of mere theatrical convenience. But surely the
Epilogue to *Henry IV* is dramatically altogether less authoritative
than the account of Falstaff's passing in the later play; and what
Shakespeare there wrote appears to me (because it is so wonderful) much less like an expedient dictated by changes in personnel
in his company than the issue of his reflections on the inner
significance of what had happened at the close of the earlier
drama. "The King has kild his heart," says Mistress Quickly as
Falstaff lies dying. "The King hath run bad humors on the
Knight," says Nym, and Pistol at once responds: "*Nym*, thou
hast spoke the right, his heart is fracted and corroborate." None
of these worthies would cut much of a figure in a witness-box;
nevertheless there is no mistaking the dramatic function of the
three consenting voices. The truth of the matter is summed
here; there follows the new king's dexterous, necessary but none
too pleasant entrapping of Cambridge, Scroope and Gray; then
comes the tremendous account of Falstaff's end—and after that
we are set for Agincourt and the regeneration and triumph of
England. It is of set purpose, then, that the rejection of Falstaff
is so resounding, so like a killing. And the reverberation of that
purpose sounds here in *Henry V*. What is it? There is an
allegorical purpose, Dover Wilson says, and with this I agree.
But I think, too, that among the "notions and associations . . .
gone out of mind" embodied in this "composite myth which
had been centuries amaking" there conceivably lies something
deeper, something which belongs equally with drama and with
magic.

When Shakespeare makes Falstaff die "ev'n just betweene Twelve and One, ev'n at the turning o' th' Tyde," he is touching a superstition, immemorial not only along the east coast of England from Northumberland to Kent but in many other parts of the world too—one shared by Dickens's Mr. Peggotty (who speaks of it expressly) and the Haidas on the Pacific coast of North America.[93] But there is more of magic about Falstaff than this; and Dover Wilson, whom the editing of Shakespeare has schooled in a fine awareness of the reverberations of English words, is more than once well on the scent. "How doth the Martlemas, your Master?" Poins asks Bardolph. And Dover Wilson comments:

> Martlemas, or the feast of St Martin, on 11 November, was in those days of scarce fodder the season at which most of the beasts had to be killed off and salted for the winter, and therefore the season for great banquets of fresh meat. Thus it had been for centuries, long before the coming of Christianity. In calling him a "Martlemas" Poins is at once likening Falstaff's enormous proportions to the prodigality of fresh-killed meat which the feast brought, and acclaiming his identity with Riot and Festivity in general.

Falstaff, in fact, is the "sweet beef," "the roasted Manning-tree ox with the pudding in his belly," who reigns supreme on the board of the Boar's Head in Eastcheap—"a London tavern . . . almost certainly even better known for good food than for good drink." There is thus from the first a symbolical side to his vast and genuine individuality; and again and again the imagery in which he is described likens him to a whole larder of "fat meat."

> 'Call in Ribs, call in Tallow' is Hal's cue for Falstaff's entry in the first great Boar's Head scene; and what summons to the choicest feast in comedy could be more apt? For there is the noblest of English dishes straightaway: Sir John as roast Sir Loin-of-Beef, gravy and all.

Is it not—I find myself asking—as if the "brawn," Sir John, "the sow that hath overwhelmed all her litter but one," were some vast creature singled out from the herd and dedicated to a high festival indeed? But such festivals commemorate more than the need to reduce stock against a winter season. They commemorate a whole mythology of the cycle of the year, and of sacrifices offered to secure a new fertility in the earth.

Now, anthropologists are always telling us of countries gone waste and barren under the rule of an old, impotent and guilty king, who must be ritually slain and supplanted by his son or another before the saving rains can come bringing purification and regeneration to the land.[94] Is not Henry IV in precisely the situation of this king? Dover Wilson avers that it is so, without any thought of magical implication:

> ... his reign and all his actions are overhung with the conscious-ness ... of personal guilt ... a fact that Shakespeare never misses an opportunity of underlining. ... We see him first at the begin-ning of act 3 crushed beneath the disease that afflicts his body and the no less grievous diseases that make foul the body of his kingdom.

Perhaps, then, we glimpse here a further reason why the rejection of Falstaff is inevitable—not merely traditionally and moralistically inevitable but symbolically inevitable as well. And this may be why, when in the theatre, we do not really rebel against the rejection; why we find a fitness too in its being sudden and catastrophic. As long as we are in the grip of drama it is profoundly fit that Hal, turning king and clergyman at once, should run bad humours on the knight, should kill his heart. For the killing carries something of the ritual suggestion, the obscure *pathos*, of death in tragedy.

I suggest that Hal, by a displacement common enough in the evolution of ritual, kills Falstaff instead of killing the king, his father. In a sense Falstaff *is* his father; certainly is a "father-substitute" in the psychologist's word; and this makes the theory of a vicarious sacrifice the more colourable. All through the play there is a strong implicit parallelism between Henry Bolingbroke and his policies and Falstaff and *his* policies; and at one point in the play the two fathers actually, as it were, fuse (like Leonardo's two mothers in his paintings of the Virgin and St. Anne), and in the Boar's Head tavern King Falstaff sits on his throne while his son Prince Henry kneels before him. And Falstaff, in standing for the old king, symbolises all the accumulated sin of the reign, all the consequent sterility of the land. But the young king draws his knife at the altar—and the heart of that grey iniquity, that father ruffian, is as fracted and corroborate as Pistol avers. Falstaff's rejection and death are very sad, but Sir James Frazer would have classed them with the Periodic Expulsion of Evils in a Material Vehicle, and discerned beneath the skin of Shakespeare's audience true brothers of the people of Leti, Moa and Lakor.[95]

If this addition of another buried significance to the composite myth of Hal and Falstaff should seem extravagant, or an injudicious striving after Morgann's "lightness of air," let it be remembered that drama, like religious ritual, plays upon atavic impulses of the mind. All true drama penetrates through representative fiction to the condition of myth. And Falstaff is in the end the dethroned and sacrificed king, the scapegoat as well as the sweet beef. For Falstaff, so Bacchic, so splendidly with the Maenads Doll and Mistress Quickly a creature of the wine-cart and the cymbal, so fit a sacrifice (as Hal early discerns) to lard the lean, the barren earth, is of that primitive and magical world upon which all art, even if with a profound unconsciousness, draws.

NOTES

[1] The significance of Pope's judgment is noticed by Peter Alexander, "Conjectural History, or Shakespeare's *Henry VIII*," *Essays and Studies*, xvi (1931), p. 96. For Johnson see *Johnson on Shakespeare*, ed. Walter Raleigh (1908), pp. 3, 33.

[2] A. C. Bradley, *Shakespearean Tragedy* (1905), p. 338.

[3] For Mrs. Thrale's experience see *Thraliana*, ed. K. C. Balderston (1942), i, 97, and for Shakespeare's Ethic merits, Elizabeth Griffith, *The Morality of Shakespeare's Drama Illustrated* (1775), pp. v, ix, 71.

[4] *Johnson on Shakespeare*, p. 58.

[5] William Archer, *The Old Drama and the New* (1923), Introduction.

[6] Tolstoy's *Shakespeare and the Drama* is reprinted by A. Maude in *Tolstoy on Art* [1924]. For Keats see the sonnet "On sitting down to read *King Lear* once again."

[7] Sigmund Freud, *Collected Papers* (1925), iv, 183. A somewhat similar view is expressed by W. B. Yeats in *The Symbolism of Poetry* (*Essays*, 1924, pp. 195 ff.): "The purpose of rhythm, it has always seemed to me, is to prolong the moment of contemplation, the moment when we are both asleep and awake, which is the one moment of creation, by hushing us with an alluring monotony, while it holds us waking by variety, to keep us in that state of perhaps real trance, in which the mind liberated from the pressure of the will is unfolded in symbols. . . . So I think that in the making and in the understanding of a work of art . . . we are lured to the threshold of sleep, and it may be far beyond it, without knowing that we have ever set our feet upon the steps of horn or of ivory."

[8] That it is necessary to read as poetically as we can is a point made by A. C. Bradley in *Oxford Lectures on Poetry* (1909), p. 4.

[9] G. Wilson Knight, *The Shakespearian Tempest* (1940 ed.), p. 7.

[10] Elizabeth Montagu, *An Essay on the Writings and Genius of Shakespear* (1769), pp. 8, 11. For Johnson see Boswell's *Life*, ed. Hill (1887), ii, 88, and *Johnson on Shakespeare*, p. 31; and for Dryden *Essays*, ed. W. P. Ker (1900), i, 80.

[11] Edward Taylor, *Cursory Remarks on Tragedy, on Shakespear, and on certain French and Italian Poets* (1774), pp. 37–8. The passage is cited in R. W. Babcock's *The Genesis of Shakespeare Idolatry* (1931), to which I also owe the references to Horace Walpole, Steevens and Malone.

[12] Gustav Rümelin, *Shakespearestudien*. I have used the second edition (1874).

[13] Bridges's essay was first printed in 1907 in vol. x of the "Stratford" Shakespeare, reprinted privately in America in 1926, and published in England in 1927 as vol. i of *Collected Essays*. In quoting from the essay I have neglected certain peculiarities of spelling and typography. But Bridges said that he was then (1927) more interested in these than in the matter.

[14] A. C. Bradley in "Shakespeare's Theatre and Audience," *Oxford Lectures on Poetry*, p. 362.

[15] For Shakespeare's joke see E. K. Chambers, *William Shakespeare*, (1930), ii, 212; and for the remark attributed to John Shakespeare see p. 247.

[16] For argument that much of Lucio's part in *Measure for Measure* is the product of expansion of the text by a hand other than Shakespeare's see J. Dover Wilson in the "New Shakespeare" edition of the play (1922). On *Romeo and Juliet* see L. Pearsall Smith, *On Reading Shakespeare* (1933), p. 17; H. Granville-Barker, *Prefaces to Shakespeare, Second Series* (1930), p. 10; and J. Dover Wilson, "The Elizabethan Shakespeare," *Proceedings of the British Academy*, 1929.

[17] I here draw upon the substance of a paper printed in *Review of English Studies*, xxi (1945), 264–70.

[18] Cf. P. V. Kreider, "Gloucester's Eyes," *Shakespeare Assn. Bulletin*, 1933, viii.

[19] H. Granville-Barker, *Prefaces to Shakespeare, First Series* (1927), p. 179.

[20] Edmund Blunden, *Shakespeare's Significances* (1929), p. 18.

[21] G. Wilson Knight, *The Wheel of Fire* (1930), pp. 186-8.

[22] Caroline Spurgeon, *Shakespeare's Imagery and What it Tells Us* (1935), p. 338.

[23] G. Wilson Knight, *The Shakespearian Tempest*, p. 218.

[24] Levin Schücking, *Character Problems in Shakespeare's Plays* (1922), p. 19.

[25] W. Raleigh, *Shakespeare* (1907), p. 27.

[26] Schücking's suggestion is made in "The Baroque Character of the Elizabethan Tragic Hero," *Proc. Brit. Acad.*, 1938, p. 87.

[27] J. Addington Symonds, *Shakspere's Predecessors in the English Drama* (1884), p. 370.

[28] The essay is R. W. Chambers's *King Lear* (1940).

[29] The essay is again by R. W. Chambers, *The Jacobean Shakespeare and "Measure for Measure," Proc. Brit. Acad.*, 1937.

[30] It would appear to be just such men as Angelo, cold to common solicitations and believing themselves substantially insensible to sexual satisfactions, who are liable to the kind of aberration depicted: sudden uncontrollable lust for a woman specially circumstanced, or habited. This is certainly morbid; but psychology insists that responses like Angelo's shade into "normal" if irrational varieties of "love at first sight." Cf. Havelock Ellis, *Psychology of Sex: a Manual* (1933), pp. 130, 144, etc.

[31] J. Middleton Murry, *Shakespeare* (1936), p. 393.

[32] I quote from Quiller-Couch's introduction to the play in the "New Shakespeare" (1931), p. xvi.

[33] For Horace Walpole's opinion see H. H. Furness, *The Winter's Tale* (a New Variorum Shakespeare), pp. 310–11; and for Lady Martin see p. 366.

[34] The description of the poet's mind is from S. L. Bethell, *Shakespeare and the Popular Dramatic Tradition* (1944), p. 115.

[35] The quotation is from Eliot's introduction to Bethell's book.

[36] The passages from Freud will be found in *Collected Papers* (1924), ii, 232 ff.

[37] The recent editor is Dover Wilson. See his notes on I, ii, 237 and II, i, 52 in the "New Shakespeare" edition.

[38] That Shakespeare is chiefly concerned to achieve "steep tragic contrast" is the opinion of E. E. Stoll. I examine it in Chapter V.

[39] H. Granville-Barker, *Prefaces to Shakespeare, Fourth Series* (1945), p. 157n.

[40] On Falstaff Edward Taylor would have agreed with Bridges. He condemns Shakespeare as "fond of exposing disgusting as well as beautiful figures" and declares: "Let it not be advanced as a merit, let it not be urged even as an excuse, that Shakespear followed nature in the busy walks of men, that he presented her, as he found her, naked and unadorned: for there are parts of nature that require concealment." And Taylor's conclusion is convinced: "And is then poor Shakespear to be excluded from the number of good tragedians? He is." (Op. cit., pp. 39, 50, 51.)

[41] For Gabriel Harvey's opinion of *Hamlet* see E. K. Chambers, op. cit., ii, 197. I have lost my reference to the attitude of the Russian peasants. Their response would have gratified Tolstoy.

[42] I here reproduce part of a paper printed in *The Modern Language Review*, xl (1945), 166–73.

[43] I am indebted here to Sir Mark Hunter's "Politics and Character in Shakespeare's *Julius Caesar*" (*Trans. Royal Soc. Lit.*, x, 1931), surely one of the best essays on the play.

[44] H. Granville-Barker, *Prefaces to Shakespeare, First Series*, p. 83.

[45] Swinburne's description of Brutus is in *A Study of Shakespeare* (1879), p. 159.

[46] For Granville-Barker on Polonius see *Prefaces to Shakespeare, Third Series* (1937), p. 253.

[47] Mr. Wopsle's *Hamlet* is described in chap. xxxi of *Great Expectations*.

[48] The relevance of the passage on the King's Evil to the master-themes of the play is distinguished by L. C. Knights in *How Many Children Had Lady Macbeth?* (1933).

[49] H. Granville-Barker, *Prefaces to Shakespeare, Second Series* (1930), p. 127.

[50] See Franz Boas's essay *apud* Ruth Benedict, *Patterns of Culture* (1934). To this book, and to Margaret Mead's *Sex and Temperament in Three Primitive Societies* (1935), I am indebted here.

[51] *Oxford Lectures on Poetry*, p. 247.

[52] Doris and Dusty are to be met in T. S. Eliot's *Sweeney Agonistes* (1932).

[53] Lascelles Abercrombie, "A Plea for the Liberty of Interpreting," *Proc. Brit. Acad.*, 1930, p. 137. This is the best examination known to me of historical realism in Shakespeare studies.

[54] M. Arnold, *Essays in Criticism* (1865), Preface.

[55] This paper is printed in *Review of English Studies*, xix (1943), 25.

[56] I take the translation from the New Variorum edition of *Macbeth*.

[57] Francis Bacon, *Of the Proficience and Advancement of Learning* (1605), Book II, iv, 1.

58 E. K. Chambers, in the " Warwick" edition of *Macbeth*, p. 19.

59 T. Reik, *The Unknown Murderer*, International Psycho-Analytical Library (1936), pp. 42–3. I am indebted in this section to Mr. Michael Innes's *Strange Intelligence*, an imaginary conversation included in a volume published in 1948 by Messrs. Secker and Warburg.

60 The observation on "our unknown selves" occurs in a leading article in the *Times Literary Supplement*, 1931, p. 554.

61 T. S. Eliot, *Selected Essays* (1932), p. 116.

62 *Johnson on Shakespeare*, p. 183.

63 From this point I include some notice of other writings of Stoll's on *Othello*.

64 I am indebted in this paragraph to Maud Bodkin, *Archetypal Patterns in Poetry* (1934).

65 T. S. Eliot, *Selected Essays*, p. 130.

66 The critic citing Rousseau and Blake is L. Kirchbaum, *English Literary History*, December 1944.

67 The writer attacking Bradley is F. R. Leavis in "Diabolic Intellect and the Noble Hero," *Scrutiny*, December 1937, vi, 3.

68 H. Granville-Barker, *Prefaces to Shakespeare, Fourth Series*, p. 156n. Dr. Ernest Jones has pointed out to me that, from the psycho-analytic point of view, *Othello* like *The Winter's Tale* turns upon sexual inversion, there being no possible motive for Iago's behaviour in destroying Othello and Desdemona except the rancour of the rejected and jealous lover of the Moor. This reading does, of course, fit. It explains, for example, Iago's baseless suspicions about Othello and Emilia: Iago, like Leontes, projects upon his wife desires in himself the conscious knowledge of which he would avoid. This seems to me the best way of taking *Othello* as a thoroughly naturalistic play—which, however, I scarcely suppose it to be.

69 "The most finite of the tragedies" is Bradley's description.

70 S. T. Coleridge, *Biographia Literaria*, ed. J. Shawcross (1907), i, 202.

71 J. Middleton Murry, op. cit., p. 320.

72 H. Granville-Barker, *Prefaces to Shakespeare, Fourth Series*, p. vi.

73 The resemblances between *The Famous Victories* and Shakespeare's trilogy are detailed by B. M. Ward in *Review of English Studies* (1928), iv, 270–94. On the question of Shakespeare's possible revision of his own work see A. E. Morgan, *Some Problems of Shakespeare's "Henry IV"* (Shakespeare Association Pamphlet, 1924).

74 John W. Draper, *Review of English Studies*, viii (1932), 414–24.

75 L. C. Knights, op. cit., p. 21.

76 E. E. Stoll, *Shakespeare Studies* (1927), chap. viii.

77 Morgann's essay is reprinted in *Eighteenth Century Essays on Shakespeare*, ed. D. Nichol Smith (1903). Matthew Arnold appeared not always wholly serious to his niece, Miss Mary Augusta.

78 C. Singer, *A Short History of Science* (1941), pp. 336–8.

79 *Coleridge's Shakespearean Criticism*, ed. T. M. Raysor (1930), i, 37, 227.

80 *The Works and Life of Walter Bagehot* (1915), i, 239.

81 J. Keats, *Letters*, ed. M. Buxton Forman (1935), p. 228.

[82] Freud notes of imaginative writers their tendency "to split up their ego by self-observation into many component-egos, and in this way to personify the conflicting trends in their own mental life in many heroes." (Op. cit., iv, 180.) The work of art—and typically a tragedy—is thus analytical, and the clarification it effects allows of something the same sort of beneficial emotional discharge as should occur in the course of analytic therapy. But it may be that in taking this view Freud, like Bridges after another fashion, is unconsciously subjecting himself to "the longest tyranny that ever swayed" and considering too exclusively Aristotle's theory of catharsis. We must not neglect the probability that tragedy evinces also the simpler mechanism of the ordeal. Thomas Hardy's belief that "If way to the Better there be, it exacts a full look at the Worst" is certainly operative when we sit through *King Lear* or *Othello*.

[83] Tolstoy, loc. cit.

[84] J. Masefield, *Shakespeare* (1912), pp. 112–13.

[85] J. Dover Wilson, *The Fortunes of Falstaff* (1943).

[86] H. B. Charlton, *Shakespearian Comedy* (1938), chap. vii.

[87] The references are to Lascelles Abercrombie, op. cit., and Sir Arthur Quiller-Couch, *Shakespeare's Workmanship* (1918), chap. vii.

[88] P. Alexander, *Shakespeare's Life and Art* (1939), p. 120.

[89] E. M. W. Tillyard, *Shakespeare's History Plays* (1944), p. 291.

[90] Rowe is cited by A. Shaaber, *2 Henry IV* (a New Variorum Shakespeare), p. 584.

[91] Bradley's essay is in *Oxford Lectures on Poetry*. I have largely employed his own words.

[92] The "impartiality" of Shakespeare here is developed by John Palmer, *Political Characters of Shakespeare* (1945), p. 249.

[93] The superstition is noticed by Sir J. G. Frazer, *The Golden Bough* (abridged edition, 1922), p. 35.

[94] See F. M. Cornford, *The Origin of Attic Comedy* (1914), chap. iv, "Some Types of Dramatic Fertility Ritual," sec. 28, "The Young Man and the Old King."

[95] For Leti, Moa and Lakor see Frazer, op. cit., p. 566. I hope it will be clear that what I am here concerned with is the *multiple* significance of the Falstaff story. To assert that Falstaff "is" the sacrificial object in a fertility ritual is not in the least to deny that he "is" (a good deal less remotely indeed) the Riot of a Morality; nor, again, that he "is" a latent personality of Shakespeare's; nor, yet again, that he "is" an aspect of the human psyche in general. For notice of one interpretation in terms of this last idea see Mr. Lionel Trilling's admirable essay, "Freud and Literature," *Horizon* (September 1947), xvi, 92.

INDEX

145